COMPLETE
METALSMITH

Student Edition

Acknowledgments

So many people contributed to this book that it is impossible to mention them all. The students I've worked with in college classes and at workshops have helped clarify many of the descriptions. I owe a huge debt to the generous authors whose books have been so valuable in my professional life.

With each new edition of this book I have been privileged to call upon a wider circle of colleagues, too many, in fact, to name. I would be remiss, however, if I did not specifically thank these talented innovators for their help: Chuck Evans, Gary Griffin, and Bob Ebendorf reviewed the original manuscript in 1980. Their wisdom rolls through the subsequent editions. Peter Handler, John Pirtle, Paula Dinneen, Will Earley, and John Cogswell have given valuable advice, as have Alan Revere, Charles Lewton-Brain, Kate Wolf, Blain Lewis, Bill Seeley, David LaPlantz, Steve Midgett, Tina Rath, Kevin Whitmore, and Darnall Burks.

For editorial insight, hats off to Abby Johnston, Jenny Hall, Katie Kazan, Margery Niblock, and Kate O'Halloran. And thanks to Mark Jamra, for his careful typographic eye, and this lovely font. Wyatt Wade of Davis Publications has supervised all three revisions of the book, consistently offering a blend of support and sound judgment. And most of all, I especially want to thank my family: Jay, Jobie, and Jeff.

Tim McCreight
Brunswick, Maine

Committed to protecting our environment through reforestation, offsets, and education.

COMPLETE
METALSMITH

Tim McCreight

Brynmorgen Press

I hear and I forget.
I see and I remember.
I do and I understand.

—

Chinese proverb

The Complete Metalsmith is also available as an iBook

A digital edition for iPad and Macintosh computers is available through the Apple iBooks Store. Features include:

• the full text of the 312-page Professional Edition
• video clips
• calculators for studio math
• a glossary and onboard dictionary
• a universal search option
• ability to make notes, bookmark and send pages by email

Contents

Introduction

This book represents years of intensive research and experimentation. Information from hundreds of sources has been collected, distilled, and illustrated. It is intended to be both a text and a tool, a blend of instruction and reference. Like other tools, its value increases as you bring to it your own perceptions and skills. It is designed to make the information easily accessible, and built to stand up to years of benchside use.

This book was originally published in 1980, then revised and enlarged in 1991. With the coming of a new century, plans were made to revise it again. The challenge we faced was to deal with two elements that were important to the book's success—thoroughness and ease of use. The question became, "How can we make it basic and advanced at the same time?" The solution was to create two editions, each with its own virtues. This Student Edition gives solid, must-have information that is appropriate for entry level students, hobbyists, and casual metalsmiths. The Professional Edition covers the same material, but goes into greater depth.

Metalsmithing involves some chemicals and procedures that are potentially dangerous. Great care has been taken to omit hazards where possible, and to give clear warnings wherever they apply. These will be only as effective as you make them. So, be wise.

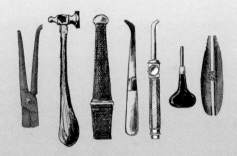

Chapter 1
Metals

Metallurgy

Crystals

Crystals move most easily within a semi-ordered structure. Crystals at a grain boundary are caught in a logjam with the result that the metal is tough and difficult to work.

annealed   work-hardened

When metal is worked, large crystals are broken into smaller ones, which creates more grain boundaries. We refer to such metal as work-hardened. A similar condition is created when metal is rapidly cooled. Because crystals do not have time to grow into an organized structure, the metal recrystallizes into many small grains.

Eventually crystals will realign themselves into an organized lattice. By heating metal we accelerate the movement of atoms and the subsequent recrystallization. This process is called annealing.

Deformation

When force is applied to a metal, it yields in a process called *elastic deformation*. If only limited stress is applied, the metal will bounce back. There will come a point, though, when the force is enough to permanently bend the metal, a process called *plastic deformation*. Each alloy has unique limits of elastic and plastic deformation.

elastic deformation

plastic deformation

Recrystallization

When a metal is heated to its melting point it loses its crystalline organization and becomes fluid. When the heat source is removed and the metal cools, it reestablishes its crystal pattern, starting with the first areas to cool. Many clusters of crystals start to form simultaneously, all having the same order but not necessarily the same orientation.

As crystals form, they bump into one another, forming irregular grains. The red line traces grain boundaries.

Annealing

Annealing is the process of reducing stress within metal by heating it to a prescribed temperature with a torch or kiln. Quench a piece in water to cool, then slide it into pickle to dissolve surface oxides. In its annealed state, the crystal arrangement contains irregularities called vacancies. These facilitate crystal movement and so contribute to malleability.

For most jewelry metals, heat to a dull red and quench as soon as the redness disappears.

Gold

- Gold was probably the second metal to be worked by early humans, being discovered after copper. Quality gold work can be found from as early as 3000 B.C.
- If all the gold ever found (about 20,000 tons) were cast into a single ingot, it would make only a 20-yard cube.
- One ounce of gold can be flattened to a sheet that will cover 100 square feet, or drawn to a wire almost a mile long.
- Gold can be made into a foil that is less than five millionths of an inch thick. At this point it is semi-transparent.

Gold	Au
Melting point	1945° F
	1063° C
Hardness	2–2.5
Specific gravity:	
Cast	19.23
Worked	19.29–19.34
Atomic weight	197.2

Alchemist symbols for gold.

Gold-filled

This term refers to a material on which a layer of gold has been bonded by fusing. The resulting ingot is rolled or drawn to make sheet and wire. A standard practice is to clad the base with 10% (weight) 12K gold. Since 12K is half pure, this means that the final result, if it were melted down and assayed, would equal 1/20 or 5% pure gold. This is marked as 1/20 GF. This technique has two advantages over plating: a thicker layer of gold can be achieved, and the gold is denser because it has been worked. The term rolled gold refers to a similar material that has only half as thick a gold layer: 1/40.

What karat is it?

Determining karat requires a testing kit:
- nitric acid and aqua regia
- metal samples of known karat
- touchstone (slate or ceramic)

Rub the object to be tested on the stone (called "touching") to leave a streak. Make a parallel line on the stone with one of the test needles. Flood both marks with acid and observe the reactions. When the two streaks change color at the same rate, a match has been made. Nitric acid is used for low-karat golds and aqua regia is used for high karats.

Silver

Silver Ag	
Melting point	1763° F
	961.7° C
Hardness	2.5 +/-
Specific gravity	10.5
Atomic weight	107.88

Sterling.925	
Melting point	1640° F
	893° C
Specific gravity	10.41

Sterling

Sterling is the alloy most commonly used in jewelrymaking and silversmithing. It was adopted as a standard alloy in England in the 12th century when King Henry II imported refiners from an area of Germany known as the Easterling. Coin silver, an alloy once used in currency, contains more copper than sterling (10% to 20%). It melts at a lower temperature than sterling and is more likely to tarnish. A 90% alloy was used in U.S. coins until 1966 but now no silver is used in any U.S. coin. An alloy popular in the Far East uses 90–93% silver and the balance zinc, producing a metal with a low melting point and a bright, white shine.

In recent years a number of alternate sterling alloys have been patented. Most replace a small amount of the copper with a metal that is less likely to oxidize such as tin, germanium, zinc, or platinum. These alloys are commonly used in casting and are available as sheet and wire. A popular brand is Argentium Silver.

Argyria

Argyria, a condition caused by ingesting silver, is evidenced by a blue or blue-gray skin color. Until the 1950s silver was used in several medicines, and it is still sold as a miracle cure for such ailments as leprosy, plague, and anthrax. In 1999 the Food and Drug Administration prohibited sellers of colloidal silver preparations from making claims about health benefits.

Electrolytic Cleaning

This kitchen version of electrostripping is especially useful for removing tarnish from flatware. Line a pot with aluminum foil and stir in ¼ cup of baking soda, a pinch of salt, and a little liquid soap with enough water to cover the objects. Set the sterling in the pot, bring the mix to a simmer and allow it to stand for at least 20 minutes. The oxides will be transferred to the aluminum, which you'll see is darkened. Throw that away and wash the silver before using it.

Copper

History

Copper was probably the first metal to be put to use by our ancestors and remains important to us today. It conducts heat and electricity very well, can be formed and joined, and combines with many elements to form a broad range of alloys.

Copper	Cu
Melting point	1981° F
	1083° C
Hardness	3 +/-
Specific gravity	8.96
Atomic weight	63.5

— 8000 BC	Copper was discovered.
— 6000 BC	Egyptians used copper weapons.
— 5000 BC	Beginning of the Bronze Age.
— 3800 BC	Evidence of controlled bronze alloying.
— 2750 BC	Egyptians made copper pipes.

Copper is available in more than 100 alloys. Comprehensive data is available from:

Copper Development Association
260 Madison Avenue
New York, NY 10016
212–251–7200
www.copper.org

Commercial Copper

› Copper is sold in standard sheets 36"x 96" (3' x 8') and in coils 12 and 18 inches wide. When ordering, specify Hard, Half-hard, or Annealed.

› When copper is hot-rolled it develops a slightly rough surface. For this reason most craftspeople prefer cold-rolled material. Copper alloy #110 is a common choice.

› Copper cannot be heat-hardened, but responds to work-hardening.

Japanese Alloys

Shaku-do 0.5% to 4% gold, balance copper.
Melting point 1968–1980° F (1070–1082° C).

This alloy is valued for the deep purple color achieved through oxidation.

Shibu-ichi 75% copper, 25% silver.
Melting point 1775° F (968° C).

This is a silvery pink alloy that darkens and reticulates easily.

Brass & Bronze

Yellow Brass	260
Melting point	1750° F
	954° C
Specific gravity	8.5

Jeweler's Bronze	226
Melting point	1886° F
	1030° C
Specific gravity	8.7

Brass Facts

> Brass is an alloy of copper and zinc and it can achieve a wide range of properties and colors.

> The practical limit of zinc in a copper alloy is 42%. Beyond this, the alloy becomes too brittle for most uses.

> Low zinc brasses that contain up to 20% zinc are grouped under the term "gilding metals."

> Brass is mildly antibacterial.

> The bronze of antiquity was a mix of 10–20% tin with the balance being copper. Today the term bronze refers to any tin-bearing brass or golden-colored brass.

> To distinguish brass from bronze, dissolve a small sample in a 50/50 solution of nitric acid and water. Tin is indicated by the white precipitate, metastannic acid.

Common Alloys

Gun Metal
Historically an alloy of 88% copper, 10% tin, and 2% zinc, it was used to cast cannons and large industrial products.

Pinchbeck
An alloy of about 83% copper and 17% zinc invented by the English watchmaker Christopher Pinchbeck in England around 1700. It resembles gold and was used to make costume jewelry and inexpensive accessories. By extension, the word has come to mean "cheap imitation."

Nordic Gold
Alloy of 89% copper, 5% aluminum, 5% zinc, and 1% tin that is used for euro coins.

Bell Metal
An alloy of roughly 80% copper and 20% tin, used for, you guessed it, bells. It makes a rich tone when allowed to vibrate but is notoriously brittle when the blows are confined. For proof, visit Independence Hall in Philadelphia.

Nickel & Aluminum

Nickel	Ni
Melting point	2651° F
	1445° C
Specific gravity	8.9
Atomic weight	58.69

Aluminum	Al
Melting point	1220° F
	660° C
Specific gravity	2.7
Atomic weight	26.97

Nickel Silver

Copper	60%
Nickel	20%
Zinc	20%

The term "nickel silver" refers to several alloys with roughly the proportions shown above. The alloy was originally developed in the Far East and came to be known as Paktong (a.k.a. Pakton, Pakfong, Paitun, Baitong, Baitung, and other derivations). Other names include Alpacca, Electrum, Stainless NS, and Nevada Silver. Nickel silver gained in popularity after 1840 when electroplating created a need for an inexpensive silver-colored substrate. This origin can still be seen in the abbreviation EPNS which stands for electro-plated nickel silver.

This metal is used in jewelry because of its low cost and generally favorable working properties. It can be forged, stamped, soldered, and polished. Though it can be cast, its high melting point and tendency to oxidize make casting difficult.

Common Alloys

Other alloys that contain nickel are Monel Metal, Nichrome, and Nickel Alloy #752.

Properties

Aluminum is the most abundant metallic element on the planet, making up 8% of the earth's crust. Because of its light weight, resistance to corrosion and ability to alloy well, it is used structurally (buildings, aircraft, cars), as architectural trim (siding), and in functional objects like cookware. It is the second most malleable and sixth most ductile metal. It is usually found in bauxite as an oxide called alumina: Al_2O_3.

Joining

Aluminum can be soldered and joined only with special solders, many of which are sold with their own flux. Welding can be done with 43S or #717 wire used with #33 flux. Check with your supplier for detailed information. Welding is made easier with a TIG (tungsten inert gas) welder, but can be achieved with gas/oxygen systems.

Anodizing

This is a process of electrically causing the formation of a resistant oxide film on the surface of aluminum. This porous, nonconductive layer can be colored with dyes.

White Metals

Britannia Metal	
Melting point	563° F
	295° C
Specific gravity	7.4

Health & Safety

The fumes produced by these metals are potentially unhealthy. Lead can be absorbed through the skin. Wash after handling any lead-bearing alloy.

White Metals

The term "white metals" refers to several malleable, gray-colored metals and alloys with low melting points. These are also called *easily fusible alloys, pot metal,* and *type metal*, the latter coming from the use of these alloys in making printers type.

Because of their low melting points, white metals can be melted with almost any torch or on a kitchen stove. Melting is best done in a small-necked crucible or ladle to help reduce oxidation. Protect the metal from oxygen during melting with a coating of olive oil, linseed oil or lard. These float on the surface of the melt so the metal will slide out from underneath when the metal is poured.

Pewter

Pewter, as used in antiquity and associated with colonial America, was an alloy of lead and tin. In the late 1700s a substitute alloy was developed in England and named Britannia Metal. Today the words pewter and Britannia are used interchangeably and usually refer to an alloy of 91% tin, 7.5% antimony, and 1.5% copper.

Pewter can be sawn, soldered, fused, formed and cast. Keep separate tools for pewter and don't let filings accidentally mix with silver or gold. Finishing can be done with fine steel wool and a mix of lampblack (soot) and kerosene blended to a paste. Fine steel wool (4/0) also leaves a pleasant finish.

Contamination

When heated above their melting points, white metals will burn pits into gold, platinum, silver, copper, and brass. Use separate files and soldering tools to keep these metals away from each other.

Removal

To remove white metal that is fused onto sterling or gold, file, scrape, and sand to remove as much of the white metal as possible, then allow the work to soak in this solution overnight.

> 3 oz. glacial acetic acid
> 1 oz. hydrogen peroxide

Iron & Steel

Mild Steel
Melting point   2759° F
                     1515° C
Specific gravity   7.86

Iron   Fe
Melting point   1535° F
                     2793° C
Specific gravity   7.9
Atomic weight   55.85

Hardening Steel

Not all steel alloys can be hardened; only steels with 1.5% to 3.0% carbon will work. Hardening is a two-step process. First, heat the object to a bright red (called the *critical temperature*) and quench it in the appropriate media, most commonly oil. This leaves the steel in a hard but brittle condition. In the second step, called *tempering*, heat the steel to temperatures between 400–600° F (200–315° C), depending on the desired balance between hardness and flexibility. An alternate method, called *case-hardening*, diffuses carbon into the outer layers of mild steel to create a thin shell that can be hardened.

0.15–0.3% carbon	mild (low) carbon steel	cannot be hardened
0.3–0.5% carbon	medium carbon steel	used for tools
0.5–1.6% carbon	high carbon steel	specialty tools
> 2.5% carbon	malleable iron	for cast and machined parts

Properties

Iron is the world's most widely used metal. It can be alloyed with a wide range of elements to produce many diverse properties. Iron ore usually contains sulfur, phosphorus, silicon, and carbon. When all but 3–4% carbon has been smelted out, the resulting metal is poured into ingots and called cast iron or pig iron. Further refining is necessary to make a steel of good working qualities.

Metals Used for Steel Alloys

> Chromium increases corrosion resistance; 10–20% is used in stainless steel.

> Manganese increases hardenability and tensile strength.

> Molybdenum increases corrosion resistance; high temperature strength.

> Tungsten forms hard abrasion-resistant particles called tungsten carbide. It is used for cutting edges.

Reactive Metals

Titanium	Ti	Niobium	Nb
Melting point	3047° F	Melting point	4474° F
	1675° C		2468° C
Specific gravity	4.5	Specific gravity	8.57
Atomic weight	47.9	Atomic weight	92.91

Reactive Metals

This term refers to a group of six tough, gray metals that are lightweight, have a high melting point, and are resistant to corrosion. In order of importance, they are titanium, niobium, tantalum, zirconium, tungsten, and hafnium. The first two are of interest to jewelers principally because of the colors produced by their oxidation films. The others are included in this group by scientists but are less important to jewelers.

Working Properties

Titanium and niobium cannot be soldered or annealed in the jeweler's studio but both metals lend themselves to all other traditional processes. They can be drilled, filed, drawn stamped, or raised, with conventional tools. Pure titanium is ductile and shows low thermal and electrical conductivity. It is twice as dense as aluminum and half as dense as iron. Its resistance to corrosion, combined with light weight and toughness, make it well-suited to use in prosthetics. It is added to steel to reduce grain size, to stainless to reduce carbon content, to aluminum to refine grain development, and to copper to harden it.

Titanium

Titanium is the ninth most abundant element in the earth's crust and can be found in most rocks, clay, and sand. It was first identified in 1791 but has been commercially viable only since 1947 when the Kroll refining process was invented. Titanium dioxide is a white powder used in paints and enamels.

Niobium

Pure niobium is soft and ductile and polishes to look like platinum. It is more plentiful than lead and less common than copper. Niobium is extremely ductile. This property can be a drawback for applications where strength is required.

When this metal was first discovered in 1801 it was called *columbium*, but it was rediscovered and renamed in 1844.

Chapter 2
Tools

Handtools

Anyone reading this book already knows about tools, knows about the timeless and universal appeal of the Right Tool. The handtools of our field impart a wisdom that traces its roots not to brilliant thought but to a genius of touch.

Value in handtools falls into several categories: design, quality, and spirit. The first two are somewhat objective, while the last is clearly up to you. Duke Ellington said about music, "If it sounds good, it is good," and the same thing applies here. If it feels good and works well, it's the right tool for the job.

Rulers
• Work in lighting that does not cast shadows.
• Do not take measurements from the end of a ruler. It could be worn and therefore inaccurate.
• The smallest division of any ruler is printed near one end.

Degree Gauge
In this spring-activated tool, the size of the opening at the top is indicated by the scale at the bottom.

Gauge Plate
This is a thick piece of steel cut with slots of specific size. It measures both sheet and wire

in the Brown and Sharpe system (also called American Wire Gauge, AWG). The other side often shows thousandths of an inch.

To use a gauge plate, find the slot that makes a snug fit, but don't distort the metal by jamming it in. Be careful not to measure where the edge has been thinned by planishing, or thickened by shears.

Dividers
In addition to making circles like a compass, the dividers can be used to hold a measurement for quick reference. Another use is to lay out parallel lines by dragging one leg of the tool along the edge of a piece of metal.

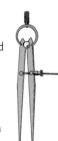

Sliding Calipers

A casual tool like this brass model should not be used for extreme precision, but it is handy for quick reference. Other sliding calipers are equipped with digital readouts or precise gauges. These can be as accurate as a micrometer.

Pliers & Snips

Standard Pliers

Pliers come in several grades and a couple sizes. The word *watchmaker* indicates a smaller than average plier. Generally the higher the cost, the better the steel and manufacture. Box joints (which trap one piece inside the other) are preferred over the weaker lap joint.

Specialty Pliers

Pliers can be purchased or modified in the studio to deliver specific results. Here are a few possibilities.

❯ To make a large version of a round-nose pliers, solder short pieces of copper or brass pipe onto pliers. Some filing of the jaws might be needed to make a good fit. For softer work, epoxy short pieces of plastic pipe.

❯ Sometimes the width of pliers is not exactly the right width for a design. Solder a piece of steel, nickel silver, or brass into a notch cut in the pliers.

Ring-Forming Pliers

One of the most versatile and effective specialty pliers has one flat and one curved jaw. These have the advantage of a curved bending mandrel matched with a flat tangent face. Note how this differs from round-nose pliers, which focus energy at a single point, almost always making a dent on the convex side of a bend.

To make standard ring-forming pliers, file, then sand one jaw of a flat-nose pliers. To make a larger version, solder a curved piece of brass, nickel silver, or steel to one jaw of a large pair of pliers.

Snips

Snips cut by creating stress that breaks the molecular bonds of the material.

Side cutters: most familiar, all-purpose wire cutter.

End cutters: designed to reach into tight corners, usually more delicate, so not recommended for thick wires.

Sprue cutters: compound action device that provides increased leverage.

Saws & Files

Nomenclature

American-made files use the names rough, bastard, second cut, smooth, and super smooth. Foreign-made files (called "Swiss" files), are graded by number from oo (coarsest) to 8. American-made files that emulate high quality files are called *Swiss Pattern* files.

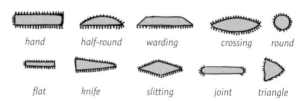

hand	half-round	warding	crossing	round

flat	knife	slitting	joint	triangle

Length

Hand files are described by the length of the working area, usually 6, 8, or 10 inches. Needle files are described by their total length.

Handles

Files should be equipped with handles to provide increased leverage and to protect your hand from being poked by the tang.

Sawframes

The principal difference between frames is the distance from the blade to the back. Smaller frames (3–4") are easier to control, but you might need a larger frame for large-scale work. Cheap

sawframes are false economy because they result in broken blades and wasted time. (This is also true of cheap sawblades.) To improve gripping comfort, slide a foam bicycle handgrip over the saw handle.

Blades

The teeth of a sawblade are angled outward alternately in a pattern called the set. This allows the corner of each tooth to engage and shear off a chip. The chip is then passed along the tooth and ejected out of the cut. When a sawblade is dull, it is usually because the set has worn away.

Blade Size

When three teeth engage the metal, the first one cuts on the left, the next tooth cuts on the right, and the third tooth keeps the blade running straight. If the blade is too small for the metal being cut, it is more likely to break. If the blade is too large, it will cut with a jerky motion.

Drills & Drilling

Safety

At the moment the cutting edge breaks through the underside of the piece being drilled, there is a tendency for the bit to snag. To avoid this, always start with a small bit and progress sequentially to larger bits. For large holes, drill a small hole, then use a saw to enlarge it.

General Rules for Drilling

> Run the drill slowly.
> Avoid wiggling.
> Keep the bit at a constant angle.
> Let the bit do the work; don't push.
> Avoid creating friction heat; lubricate with beeswax, oil of wintergreen or Bur-Life.

Drills

Pin Vise

For light use, grip a bit in a pin vise or glue it into a dowel. The tool will be more comfortable to use if it has a freely rotating knob on top, like the example shown here on the right.

Electric

Many jewelers use electric or battery powered drills or flexible shaft machines to drill holes. While these are hard to beat for ease, care must be taken not to run them too fast. Whenever possible, a drill press is preferred over a handheld drill because it guarantees a perpendicular angle of attack.

Step Bit

A step bit is a single tool that makes a large hole without spending a lot of time changing bits. These can be purchased in several ranges, and while they are expensive, they can pay for themselves in saved time... and saved fingers.

Drill Bit Styles

 Twist

 Core

 Pump

 Pearl

 Spade

Hammers & Mallets

Hammers

The heart of the metalsmith's shop is in the hammers. In fact the word "smith" is derived from the verb "to smite" which means "to hit." While only a couple hammers are needed to get started, most smiths collect specialized hammers as their shops grow. Metalworking hammers can be bought new, but many smiths acquire and alter old hammerheads to suit their needs.

Mallets

Tools in this family will bend metal without stretching or marring it. Probably the most popular material for mallets is treated rawhide. Other choices include wood, horn, fiber, plastic, and rubber. A popular material for raising mallets is Ultra High Molecular Weight (UHMW) plastic, which is rigid and inexpensive.

Planishing

Forging

Ball peen

Claw

Chasing

Riveting

Deadblow Mallets

Most hammers bounce back, a phenomenon that makes the blow seem alive. This style of mallet is designed to kill the recoil, hence the name. A deadblow mallet has a hollow interior partially filled with sand or small pieces of a heavy metal like steel or lead. A split second after the blow is delivered, this mobile weight slams against the recoil and cancels it out.

Bench Accessories

Bench Pin

Any hardwood can be used to make a bench pin. This shape is a common starting place, but in practice the pin is filed, drilled, and carved to meet specific needs. You might find you want different interchangeable pins to meet a variety of specific needs.

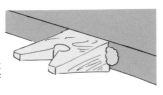

Avoid drilling holes in the bench pin because they trap metal and eventually make the surface irregular. Keep a block of wood handy for drilling. An exception to this is a few well-placed holes that make it possible to work on objects with pinbacks and similar projections.

Which Side Up?

Many people flip the pin over depending on the work being done—flat for sawing and sloped for filing. A variation on this is to create a sloped edge on the flat side.

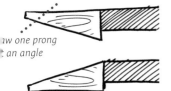

ฟ one prong
at an angle

Squares

A small square can be made from steel or brass rod. One side is thicker than the other to allow the square to rest against the item being marked. File a notch and solder the pieces together carefully. Test against a commercial square, and if it is not right, reheat and adjust. Do not try to fix by filing.

Bench Knife

A knife can be improvised by grinding and resharpening a kitchen paring knife. These can often be bought at flea markets.

Scraper

A scraper can be made by breaking off an old triangular file and grinding a point. Faces should be ground smooth and polished.

Saw Blade Holders

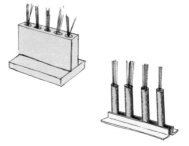

Buffing Machines

Buffing

In machine polishing, a gritty material (compound) is dragged forcefully across a surface so the high spots on the metal are worn away. In sandpaper we see the grit (media), feel the paper (vehicle), and provide the motion. In machine buffing the abrasive particles are usually too fine to see, and the vehicle is a disk made of fabric.

Tapered Spindles

Most jewelry buffing machines have a threaded tapered spindle mounted on the machine axle. These make it quick and easy to switch from one wheel to another. When buying, make sure you get a right- or left-handed spindle, depending on the setup of your motor. Also, be sure to match the diameter of the axle.

Wheels

The most commonly used wheels are made by stitching together a thick pile of sheets of woven fabric. Muslin is usually used, but wool is preferred for coarser polishing. Fabric wheels are most rigid near a layer of stitching and quite floppy away from the stitching.

Rigid felt is used, either by itself or glued onto wood, to reach precise areas.

Compounds

There are many polishing compounds and most smiths develop a favorite. Traditionally these are the most popular

Bobbing coarse, aggressive.

Tripoli medium aggressive, gives some shine.

Rouge a burnishing compound that does not remove metal but gives a shine.

Preparing & Maintaining Buffs

All wheels are sold as plain fabric, then loaded with compound, using a separate wheel for each media. Mark the wheels clearly with permanent markers or color-code them with spray paint. Before loading a fabric wheel, remove loose fibers. Turn the buffing motor on again and use a fork to rake the wheel, releasing more lint. Stop, trim as needed, and clean up the debris (which is a fire hazard).

Flexible Shaft

Flexible Shaft Machine

This relatively new member of the studio has become extremely popular because of its versatility. It is used to drill, grind, sand, carve and buff. With the addition of a reciprocating hand piece (which converts rotation to back-and-forth motion) it can be used for light hammering. What we call "flex shaft" is actually four elements.

Flex shafts are usually sold in packages with all the necessary parts, but individual components can be replaced or upgraded. Not all parts are interchangeable, so consult suppliers for details.

- **Motor** — A compact precision motor capable of speeds of 15,000–20,000 rpm (revolutions per minute). Available in $\frac{1}{10}$, $\frac{1}{8}$, $\frac{1}{5}$, $\frac{1}{4}$ and $\frac{1}{2}$ horsepower.
- **Electronic Foot Control** — A rheostat pedal that controls speed with foot pressure.
- **Shaft** — A steel spring encased in a rubber-clad sheath that carries the rotary motion of the motor to a handpiece.
- **Handpiece** — A cylinder that connects the power to a variety of tools and provides a comfortable way to hold and manipulate the tool.

Mounting

Flex shafts should be mounted at a height that allows comfortable use while allowing the shaft to hang in gentle curves.

¾" threaded steel pipe (about 2 feet) with a floor flange that can be screwed into the benchtop.

Two washers welded into a piece of angle iron. Split the bottom 2" and bend out to make legs.

Drill and saw two parallel lines in a sheet of steel, brass, or nickel silver and pound the strap portion through vise jaws.

Chuck Keys

To keep this important tool close at hand, mount it into a file handle or solder it to a screwdriver handle. Make a loop of copper or brass to attach it to a cord that is fastened to the bench.

Flex Shaft Abuse

Like any tool, the flex shaft has limitations. Because this is a rotary tool, it has the potential to wear ruts—picture a car spinning its tires in mud. Use a light touch and keep the tools moving lightly across the surface.

Folding Bench

Folding Jeweler's Bench

This compact light-duty bench comes apart into two sections, plus a drawer. The legs fold up, which makes this great for travel, shows, and really small apartments. Like the other bench shown here, this can be made from easily available commercial lumber using only a minimum of tools.

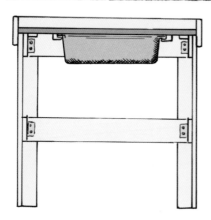

Parts List

6 pieces	1 x 3 x 8'	pine or poplar	These will become the legs, the braces, and a rim around the top.
1 piece	40" x 18"	plywood or MDF	Size is approximate—don't cut yet! See Step #6.
1 box	1¼" sheet rock screws		To preserve right angles, use wood glue along with the screws as you connect the parts.
1 plastic bin or commercial drawer			This is optional, but handy.
4 2" hinges			

Process

Read through the directions on the next page until they make sense. There is an old carpenter's adage that says, "Measure twice, cut once." Cut the legs and frame pieces, but leave the top until later.

Tools you'll need

— Square
— Handsaw
— Screwdriver
— Tape measure
— Pencil

Folding Bench

1. Make the two leg assemblies and the back frame, using a square to be sure that the pieces are at right angles. Glue and screw each joint.

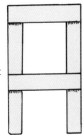

2. Lay the back frame down so the braces are facing up. Lay the leg units alongside this so they line up. Screw the hinges into place.

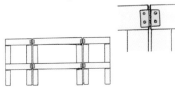

3. Fold the legs to be sure the placement is working. So far, so good, right?

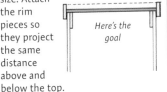

4. Lay the benchtop upside down on the floor and set the legs, also upside down, in place. The top will be held on by friction from the rim that surrounds the top.

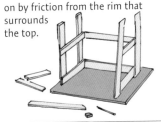

5. The top needs to be exactly as wide at the outer dimension of the legs. Mark, check, then cut the top to size. Attach the rim pieces so they project the same distance above and below the top.

Here's the goal

6. Working upside down again, attach another brace to the underside of the benchtop that lines up with the inner edge of the legs and the back.

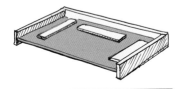

7. Buy a plastic bin, making sure that it has a rim at the top. Either cut an L-shaped piece or glue two boards together to make a track. Attach these on the underside of the bench to hold the bin.

8. Alternatively, you might find drawer sets like this in the shelving and closet section of a home remodeling store.

Basic Bench

Basic Jeweler's Bench

This bench has been designed so it can be made from easily available materials without sophisticated woodworking equipment. People with woodworking skills might use these ideas as a point of departure.

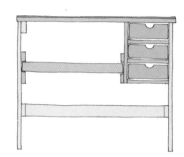

Parts List

Plywood or MDF   *inches*

A	Top (1)	48 x 24
B	Back (1)	48 x 12
C	Case sides (2)	18 x 22
D	Case ends (2)	11¾ x 22

Masonite

E	Top (1)	48 x 24
F	Sweeps (1)	29 x 22
G	Drawers (3)	11½ x 22
H	Case back (1)	13¾ x 18

Plywood or MDF   **Masonite**

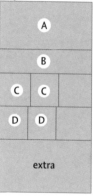

Directions

1. Cut the pieces, except for the sweeps drawer components. The dimensions given do not allow for a saw kerf. If you are using a handsaw, this space is not too important, but you should allow for an ⅛" kerf if you use a table saw.

2. Glue pieces A and AA together to make the top. Use a white glue like Elmer's or Tite-bond, set the pieces together, and clamp or weight them overnight. Traditionally, jewelers benches have a "belly hole" to allow closer access. Benches without cutouts are preferred by watchmakers. Use a saber saw after the parts have been glued together if you want a hole.

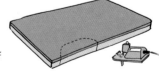

Basic Bench

. Make both leg
assemblies, using
a square to be
sure that the
pieces are at right
angles. Glue and
screw each joint.

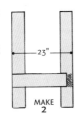

MAKE
2

4. Screw and glue the cross brace into
the leg braces. Attach the back,
allowing half of it to project above
the legs. Connect the top.

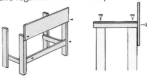

. Make a plywood box for the drawers.
Cut ¾" by ¾" strips from a 1 x 6 to
make the cleats. Nail and glue these
onto what will be the inside walls of
the box.

MAKE
2

6. Flip the bench upside down and set
the box into place. Attach it with
screws into the top and the legs.

. The drawer sides, fronts and backs
are made from a 1 x 6. Nail or screw
them together,
then glue and
nail a Masonite
panel on the
bottom. Sand
all the edges
to make them
round.

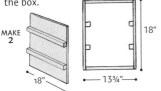

8. Cut a recess in
each drawer
front, or attach
handles. Rub
soap on the
undersides of
the drawers to
help them slide.

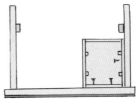

. The sweeps drawer slides between
the two cleats on each side. Attach
two on each side, and make sure
they are the same distance up from
the floor.

cleats

10. The sweeps drawer slides between
the two cleats on each side. Measure
the space and make the drawer
to match. Assemble like the other
drawers.

Cut on the
dotted lines for
better access, but don't
cut away too much or the drawer
will wobble.

Ventilation

Push vs. Pull

It takes roughly 20 times more force to pull a contaminate than to push it. A small fan behind you pushing fumes out a window is more effective than a large fan trying to draw them from within the window.

Respirators

Respirators are generally considered less effective than active ventilation since they can be a little uncomfortable and therefore are often set aside. A worthwhile respirator will have a canister or cartridge filter to chemically remove impurities and will cost at least $30 with cartridges. A paper dust mask is intended only to capture relatively large particles and should not be considered adequate protection for professional craftspeople.

> Look for the NIOSH (National Institute for Occupational Safety and Health) seal of approval.

> Choose a filter made for the danger to which you are exposed.

> Your mask must make a tight and comfortable fit. Buy the right size and have it properly fitted to your face. Do not borrow or lend a mask.

> Change filters as needed—you'll know it's time when you are aware of odors entering the mask or when intake becomes difficult. If you have trouble breathing or have a history of respiratory illness, consult a doctor at the first sign of breathing difficulty.

Replacement Air

It's true: the universe abhors a vacuum. When you pull air out of your studio, the universe finds some new air to take its place. If you supply this, the task of pulling out the old air is much easier. In other words, before you try to draw fumes away, start by supplying fresh air from across the room.

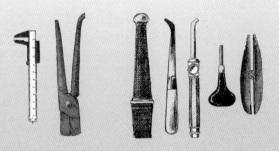

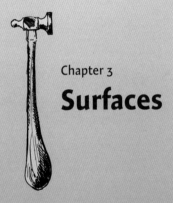

Chapter 3
Surfaces

Sanding

Overview

A polished appearance is the result of a perfectly flat surface. Under magnification, the cross section of a scratched surface looks like a series of ridges and grooves. Light is reflected between the scratches like sound being echoed in a mountain valley. A flat surface, on the other hand, bounces all the light back, which we see as a bright shine. Good finishing begins the moment you first handle metal. Store it carefully to avoid making unnecessary scratches. Don't scribe a line until you are sure of your plans.

Lights gets trapped in an irregular surface.

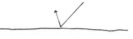

Light reflects off a flat surface, which creates what we see as shine.

Grits

100s	very coarse
200s	coarse
300s	medium
400s	fine
600s	very fine

Sanding Sticks

Wrap abrasive papers around a board or dowel to increase leverage. The cutting power of the paper depends on the force behind it.

Abrasives

For a long time, abrasive technology consisted of finding rocks that were harder than the materials to be abraded. About a century ago, synthetic abrasives such as aluminum oxide and silicon carbide were developed. These are much tougher than natural abrasives. The latest breakthrough in abrasives focuses on control of the size, shape, and distribution of particles. Somewhat surprisingly, uniformity and lack of uniformity in size have a significant effect on the results of abrasives. Microsorted abrasives are available as papers, on plastic sheets, and backed with foam rubber.

Traditional sorting establishes only a maximum size.

Micrograding sorts out both larger and smaller particles.

Buffing & Tumbling

Rules for the Buffing Machine

> Pay attention! If your mind wanders, take a break.
> Use a pinch, or breakaway, grip.
> Wear goggles. Keep long hair and loose clothing tied back.
> Work only on the lower quarter of the wheel.

Compounds

In both natural and manufactured abrasives, the finer particles resemble flour and would fly away if used in powder form. For this reason they are mixed with a thickener such as wax or tallow and formed into solid bars. These are used to coat the wheels used in machine buffing.

Polishing Cloths

Today most jewelers buy commercially produced flannel cloths, but you can still make your own the way it used to be done. Rub rouge into a soft cloth, then work it against itself to condition the fabric.

Thrumming

Polishing small spaces with string is more effective than you might think. Take up a strand, pull it taut, and stroke with tripoli or rouge to charge it. With the string pulled tight, slide the jewelry back and forth.

Tumbling

Tumbling has been used industrially for years to pulverize ore and, on a smaller scale, by lapidaries to shine cut-off pieces of gem material. In machine tumbling, hundreds of small pieces of polished metal cascade onto a piece repeatedly as both the work and tool rotate in a drum.

Media

Steel shot in several shapes provides a versatile all-purpose burnishing medium. The weight of the individual pieces ensures a reasonable impact, while the diverse shapes are likely to reach most areas. Use a pH balanced tumbling solution for best results.

Roll Printing

Roll Printing

To transfer texture and pattern from one material to another (e.g., fabric to metal), make a sandwich of the materials and pass it through the rolling mill under great pressure. This embosses the reverse image of the material into the metal.

Suggested Materials

Burlap	Screen
Sandpaper	String
Lace	Binding wire
Netting	Coarse paper
Templates	Tissue paper

Procedure

1. Anneal and dry the metal to be embossed.
2. When appropriate, anneal the texture material. An example is a paper clip.
3. Set the rollers by eye and test the tension. Adjust the rollers so the handle is difficult to move, but not so difficult that it requires two people.
4. Roll the assembly through the mill in a continuous movement so the texture is created in a single pass.

Paper Templates

Cut a paper pattern with scissors or a blade and lay it between the annealed work metal and a stiff backing sheet (such as brass). Each paper template can be used only once, but where duplicates are desired, you can photocopy the image. Each variety of paper will leave a different surface when rolled. Experiment with card stock, drawing paper and tissue.

Printing from a Metal Matrix

To create a raised pattern on the workpiece, prepare a matrix by making indentations in a metal sheet, for instance, by stamping, engraving, etching, or roll printing. A tough metal like brass or nickel silver is recommended. Follow the steps above to transfer the pattern to an annealed workpiece.

Stamping

Stamping
> Work on an anvil, preferably polished.
> Anneal the metal before starting.
> Use stock thick enough to absorb the blow.
> Grip low on the tool to increase control.
> A lower grip on the hammer handle increases power.

Letters & Numbers
Commercially made letter and number stamps can be used for surface enrichment.

Thickness
Material under the stamping tool will compact but there is a limit to how far it can go. Thicker material provides more metal within which to distribute the blow. This means that a strike on thick sheet will yield a deeper mark than the same blow on thin sheet.

Tool Design
Stamping tools can be purchased, but many smiths prefer to make their own. For hardening and tempering instructions, see the Appendix.

Top
- This area should be symmetrical and rounded so the crown is centered over the axis of the tool.
- Avoid square corners; they can deflect the tool sideways if the hammer blow is angled.
- When the top starts to mushroom over, grind, or file the edges smooth to avoid the risk of splinters being thrown off when the tool is struck.

Shaft
- Thick enough to prevent the tool from bending when struck.
- Comfortable to grasp; no sharp corners. Some people like to wrap their tools with cord or leather.
- If the stamp has a specific orientation, it is helpful to build in a tactile reference, such as a notch you can feel under your thumb.

Face
- Square to the axis.
- Flat (not crowned).
- Chamfered edges, especially on large tools; this helps the material flow outward.

Chasing

Chasing

Chasing is an ancient and often misunderstood technique used to incise lines into metal. The result can look like engraving, and the process resembles stamping, but chasing is a technique by itself. Unlike engraving, no metal is removed. Unlike stamping, the tool moves in a steady, unbroken motion. Chasing can be used to create linear patterns on flat or shaped sheet metal, and is used to sharpen details on castings.

Tips

> The tool is usually drawn toward the worker, held at such an angle that it propels itself along as it is struck.
> Use a lightweight hammer and sit comfortably. The process should be delicate and controlled.
> For small radius curves, tilt the tool more or switch to a smaller tool. Because a sharper angle may cause the tool to slip, a new tool is the better solution.
> It is important that the workpiece be securely held.
> In some applications, a raised element is created by lowering the surrounding metal.

Tools: Hammers

Though any light hammer can be used, this one has evolved over the years just for this technique. It is light enough to be used for hours, has a large face to find the tool, and fits on a comfortable pistol grip handle. The handle is thin and springy, so the hammer "spanks" the tool.

Tools: Punches

Chasing tools are made in the studio and modified by each smith to meet personal needs. The tips are precise and just sharp enough to slice into the metal without cutting through.

Close up view of the tip.   Profile view of the tip.

A gradual taper on the shank makes it easier to guide the tool.

A twisted shank provides sure grip.

Etching

Safety (yours!)

> Work only in a ventilated area.
> Wear rubber gloves, an apron, goggles, and a respirator.
> Keep baking soda handy to neutralize acid spills.
> When mixing, always add acid to water. Acid is the denser fluid of the two and will fall to the bottom of the dish and begin mixing.
> Store acids in narrow-necked glass or plastic jars with glass or plastic lids. Store in a cool dark place; never store up high.

Ferric chloride gives a clean etch on copper and brass. The work must be level, and should be suspended just below the surface of the fluid.

Process

Paint resist onto the area that is to remain at the original height. After etching, the exposed area will be lower and often textured (depending on the acid).

Or, cover the whole piece and selectively scratch the resist away.

To achieve different heights, etch a while, pull the piece out, rinse it, and apply resist over the areas that have sufficient depth then continue etching.

Traditional Etching Solutions

Most people use reagent grade and most formulas are written for this. If you have a more dilute acid, modify the formulas accordingly.

Gold	1 part nitric, 3 parts hydrochloric (aqua regia)
Sterling, Silver	1 part nitric, 3 parts water
Copper and Copper Alloys	1 part nitric, 1 part water
Aluminum	1.5 oz. ammonia, 5 gm copper sulfate, 14 oz. sodium hydroxide, 2 gallons of water
White Metals	1 part nitric, 4 parts water
Iron & Steel	2 parts hydrochloric, 1 part water

Engraving

Engraving

Engraving is a cutting process in which a steel tool called a graver or burin slices small bits of metal as it is pushed along the surface of a sheet. Gravers are made of high-quality tool steel and are usually sold in the hardened, untempered state.

Styles of Gravers

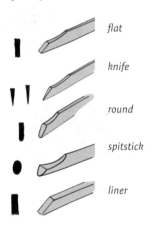

flat

knife

round

spitstick

liner

Cutting

Proper cutting involves a sliding rather than a scooping stroke. Press the graver straight down into the metal at the beginning of the cut, then slide the tool forward at a consistent depth.

To vary the width of a line, don't dig deeper, but instead, roll the graver on its side as it is pushed along. To cut a graceful curve, roll the graver and return it upright.

Grip

Hold the graver between your fingertips and along the length of your thumb. This will feel awkward at first, but it's worth getting used to. The handle should rest in the fleshy part of your palm. This is where the push comes from.

Position

Work should be at mid-chest height. When using an engraving block, a table lower than a jeweler's bench will be needed. Most engravers rely on a magnifying headset or microscope.

Engraving

Handles

Graver handles are available in several styles; choice is a matter of personal preference. Because gravers will get short with repeated sharpening, some engravers start with a short handle and later switch to a longer one to prolong use of the tool. In the EFB adjustable handle the tool is held in place by a metal sleeve. A notched piece of brass provides for the changing length of the tool.

Graver Sharpening

All engraving requires a keen, precise edge. Repeated sharpening will be needed to keep the cutting edge in shape. Although sharpening can be done by hand, an indexing device is recommended to keep each surface absolutely flat.

> To speed up the sharpening process, reduce the size of the tip. Use a grinding wheel to remove the dotted line section. Quench often during grinding to retain the temper.

> The face angle for most gravers is 45°—less for soft metals, and slightly more for hard materials. Set both a sharpening stone and the indexing jig on a smooth flat surface, such as a piece of glass or Plexiglas. Clamp the graver into the jig and rub the tool face on a stone that has a coating of light oil. Follow the coarse stone by a similar stroking on a fine stone. Continue this until all the obvious scratches are gone.

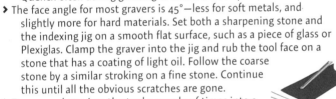

> To remove burs, jam the tool a couple of times into a block of hardwood. Polish the graver by rubbing it along a piece of fine sandpaper held on a hard flat surface. Stroke the face and belly of the tool lightly on a piece of crocus paper impregnated with rouge until they are mirrorlike.

The angle can be modified to make a tool that will cut lines of various widths. The angles do not need to be identical, but their points should meet.

Engraving machines are either electrical or pneumatic, and deliver a reciprocating action of 500–2800 strokes per minute. Air tools are slightly preferred because they are quieter and have a better maintenance record.

Inlay

Puzzle Inlay

In this process pieces are cut out to fit together in the same way that the elements of a jigsaw interlock. While considerably more tedious than lamination inlay, this method ensures an undistorted image that is visible on both front and back. Start by cutting out and refining the interior piece. Trace this with a needle and cut the whole carefully. Solder the parts together.

Lamination Inlay

In this simple process, sheets of metal are soldered together and then pressed until they are flush. This gives the appearance of an inlay. A rolling mill is helpful but not necessary for lamination inlay.

1. One piece of metal must be thicker than the desired goal and the other should be very thin, around 26 gauge. Clean the two pieces and solder them together. The bond must be complete, extending all the way to the edges. Achieve this through careful preparation and heating, not by using surplus solder. Excess solder will make a yellowish ghost image around the inlay in the finished piece.

2. After pickling and drying, pass the sheet through a rolling mill or planish it with a polished hammer until the two surfaces become flush. If rolling is to take place in both directions, anneal before changing the direction of the stretch. Lamination inlay is not recommended where specific shapes are required since distortion is inherent in the process.

3. Finish conventionally with files, paper, and buffing if desired. Subsequent soldering could spoil the effect. As a precaution, use a lower melting solder and protect the inlay with yellow ocher.

Solder Inlay

In this simple and versatile technique, flow solder into grooves made by hammering, engraving, roll printing or etching.

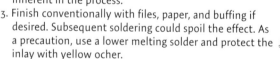

Inlaying Cane Material

Make a length of material (cane) whose cross section reveals an interesting pattern. Slice thin sections, solder to a sheet and roll this through the mill.

Reticulation

Reticulation

In this process, metal is made to draw itself into ridges and valleys, creating a unique texture. Many alloys can be made to reticulate, but an alloy of 82% silver and 18% copper yields particularly dramatic results. The buckling is the result of the different cooling rates of the two strata created in the sheet.

Process

1. Heat a piece of 18 or 20 gauge metal to 1200° F (650° C) and hold for 5 minutes. Do not use flux, since the purpose of this step is to create a layer of copper oxide. Air cool.
2. Pickle in hot fresh Sparex to remove copper oxide from the surface. This leaves a silver-rich skin.
3. After rinsing, heat as before to the same temperature, this time for at least 10 minutes. Oxygen cannot react much with the silver-rich skin so it penetrates and promotes growth of the copper oxide layer into the sheet (i.e., interior oxidation). Air cool. The sheet should be only slightly gray. Pickle as before.
4. Preheat a soldering block, then bring the sheet to red with a sharp, hot flame, then quickly pass the torch over an area, allowing it to cool. The cooling is what causes the metal to buckle. The skin may melt but try to minimize this because surface melting softens the sharpness of the ridges and diminishes the effect. Allow the piece to lose redness before quenching.
5. Reticulated metal can be soldered, colored, and finished like its original stock. Because it is brittle, extensive forming is not recommended. The copper oxide layer is porous and soaks up solder so you should burnish edges before soldering.

Materials

Because copper plays an important role in reticulation, higher copper content generally enhances the results. 14K yellow or rose gold will work better than 14K green or white or any color of 18K. An alloy of 820 parts silver (balance copper) produces especially dramatic results. You can make your own reticulation silver by adding 10% copper (by weight) to sterling, or it can be purchased from Hauser & Miller Inc. or Hoover and Strong (see Appendix for addresses).

Mokumé

Mokumé

Mokumé-gane (MO-ku-may), is a Japanese technique in which layers of contrasting metals are used to create a multicolored wood-grain effect. Sheets of copper, sterling, fine silver, gold, and other jewelry alloys are either fused or soldered together, then hammered with punches to create an irregular topography. This is filed off to reveal a pattern, which can be either random or planned.

Diffusion

Diffusion creates a seamless block that can be treated like any other metal mass.

1. Make panels flat, clean, and similar in length, width, and thickness.
2. Wrap the stack in stout binding wire and heat it with a large bushy flame. Once you begin, keep the flame on the metal—taking it off invites oxygen into the stack.
3. Heat the stack evenly until you see the surfaces shimmer. Press down on the stack with a steel rod, starting at the center and moving outward to the edges. Continue to heat until the entire stack is glowing with one color. The layers will seem to disappear.
4. Air cool, examine, and repeat if needed.

Soldering

Soldering is handy when a small piece of mokumé is needed.

1. Flatten and clean small sheets (1" square) of several metals.
2. Roll pieces of hard sheet solder to make them as thin as possible.
3. Flux each panel on both sides and stack the alternating colors with a piece of solder between each one. This pile can have 3 to 9 sheets, not counting the solder.
4. Heat the whole pile with a large bushy, reducing flame until you see the solder flow at the seams.
5. Air cool. Do not quench, especially in pickle.
6. Roll the sheet to half its original thickness, clean the exposed surfaces, and cut the piece in half. Solder these two pieces, which will double the number of layers. Again, air cool. Repeat until achieving 10–30 layers.

Creating the Pattern

Whatever method you choose to create a billet, after all the work, you will have a rather boring stack of metals; a sort of miniature plywood. Roll or forge the laminate to 18 or 20

gauge and anneal. Set it on a medium soft surface and strike it with small punches to create a bumpy sheet. File, sand, and polish the metal using conventional techniques. The pattern will be faint until the mokumé has been colored.

Granulation

Granulation

This demanding process uses a delicate, solderless bonding to attach small pieces to a surface. The technique relies on a diffusion process related to *eutectic bonding*. A small amount of metal (usually copper) is introduced to the contact area, and when appropriate heat is reached, an alloy of a lower melting point is created at the point of contact.

Making Granules in a Kiln

1. Line a steel can with about ¾" of powdered charcoal.
2. Sprinkle tiny chips of metal on this layer, then build up alternate layers of charcoal and metal chips.
3. Set the can into a kiln until it glows red hot and hold it at this heat for about 15 minutes. Ventilate well.
4. Air cool the can, then pour the contents into a dish of water.

Making Granules with a Torch

1. Cut the metal into chips and sprinkle them onto a clean flat charcoal block.
2. Hold the block in a gloved hand about 12" above a dish of water. Hold the block at an angle that allows each granule to roll off as it draws into a sphere.

To introduce additional metal to create the low-melting alloy that will create the bond, coat the granules with a mixture of a metallic salt and a glue that contains carbon. Use Handy flux mixed with antimony trioxide, copper chloride, verdigris, or copper nitrate. Another method is to coat the granules with copper by placing them in saturated pickle.

Firing

Set the granules onto clean metal with tweezers or a brush. Avoid a single line of granules if possible because it is weak. Dip the granules in the flux/glue mix before applying, but pick up excess liquid with a tissue. Allow the work to dry thoroughly before applying the torch.

With a broad flame, bring the whole piece to bright red. Remove the torch when the joints flash. To supply heat from both above and below the work, place work in a trinket kiln.

Patina

Patina Thinking

Some metals, such as pure gold or platinum, do not react to the chemicals around them, but they are the exception. Most metals react with their environment, which is what produces their color. A few metals, such as tin, oxidize to a stable film, but most metals will continue to change. People who are uncomfortable with change might not enjoy patinas—random and transient effects are inherent to the materials.

Preparation

Always clean metal before any coloring operation. The best way to achieve this is to avoid greasy materials like steel wool and buffing compounds in the first place. Alternate finishing materials include pumice, sandpaper and Scotch-Brite.

Preservation

To minimize changes in patinas, metals are sealed off from their environment. A hard film such as lacquer will resist marring but can eventually be chipped away. A soft film such as wax is more likely to be vulnerable to wear but will probably just smudge across the protected surface.

Application Methods

Immersion

This method is standard practice when coloring sterling with liver of sulfur. Clean the work and dip it into a patina solution. Rinse in water and reimmerse as needed. The results will be affected by the temperature of the metal, the temperature of the solution, and the duration of immersion.

Spray

Spritz the work with patina solution, sometimes at room temperature and sometimes with the addition of heat.

- Put the work on a turntable to facilitate even coating.
- Set a cardboard box behind it to catch overspray.
- Place a fan behind you to direct spray away from yourself.
- To avoid overheating, use a hair dryer rather than a torch.

Brushing

Some patinas can be applied like paint. Use brushes, sponges, wads of cheesecloth, and other improvised tools to dab solution onto the metal. To thicken patina solutions so they can be applied without running, mix cornstarch or flour into a liquid patina solution to make a thick paste. An interesting halo effect is sometimes created by fumes escaping from the lump.

Patina

Liver of Sulfur	Dissolve a rice-size piece of liver of sulfur in a cup of warm water. Dip and quickly rinse in water. Repeat to slowly create a sequence of colors.	**Silver alloys:** golden > scarlet > blue > plum > black **Copper:** gray > purple > black
Commercial Oxidizer e.g., Silver Black, Black Max, etc.	On gold, steel is required to create the reaction. Use a bit of steel wool held in tweezers as a brush. These proprietary solutions are available through most jewelry supply companies. Avoid contact with your skin and eyes.	Black—no transition colors
Green Patina #1	1 part ammonium chloride (1%) 6 parts copper sulfate (11%) 60 parts water (88%) *Apply the solution to the metal and allow it to dry. Repeat several layers, allowing each to dry.*	Variegated green layer
Green Patina #2	1 part zinc chloride (2%) 2 parts acetic acid (3%) 4 parts ammonium chloride (5%) 4 parts table salt (5%) 8 parts copper sulfate (10%) 60 parts water (75%) *Dissolve all ingredients together and mix well. Brush or spray onto the piece..*	Variegated green layer
Gun Bluing	Use full strength by brushing or immersion. On brass or bronze, apply the solution with steel wool. This commercial preparation is available at most sporting goods stores.	Gray > deep purple

For examples and more recipes, visit www.brynmorgen.com/resources.html

Enameling Equipment

Equipment

Enameling can be done with a torch, but most enameling is performed in a small electric kiln. This provides a clean, contained environment where heat can be sustained and measured. Modern kilns use lightweight refractory (heat-resistant) materials that can be formed over the wires that carry electric current. Older, heavier kilns are lined with bricks and reveal a wire coil that generates heat when electricity is run through it.

Stilts and Shelves

In the course of enameling, objects are set into the kiln and removed many times. A variety of racking systems have been devised to accommodate this— each enamelist will have several. Good stilts will hold objects securely while making minimal contact that might damage the enameled surface. Most stilts are made of steel alloys that resist warping and oxidizing at high temperatures.

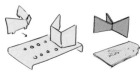

Forks

Forks are used to insert and withdraw objects from a kiln. They should be sturdy enough to avoid vibration and thick enough to slow down the conduction of heat. Most have two tines (which should fit the shelves) and a guard to shield the user's hand from the heat of the kiln. This is intentionally left loose to discourage heat transfer from one part to another.

Pyrometer

Pyrometers work by measuring what happens when two different metals are exposed to heat. This arrangement is called a thermocouple. In an analog pyrometer, this imbalanced charge pushes a hand across a dial. Because the charge is so small, the hand must be very lightweight, which is why the needles in pyrometers are almost invisibly delicate. In digital pyrometers the current difference of the thermocouple is converted to readouts, making these devices both easier to read and more durable.

Enameling

Washing Enamels

Enamels are made from crushed glass. The grinding process creates tiny flakes that can trap air and make the glass murky. To separate the flakes, put a small amount of enamel powder in a shallow dish, cover with water, and swirl the dish gently. After a few seconds, pour off the cloudy water. Repeat at least three times.

Hardness

In enameling this word refers to melting point. Soft enamels have a low melting point; enamels that fuse at higher temperatures are said to be harder.

> **Soft**   1300–1360° F
>   704–738° C

> **Medium**   1360–1420° F
>   738–771° C

> **Hard**   1420–1510° F
>   771–821° C

Counterenamel

A layer of enamel is applied to the back side of a piece to offset the difference in contraction between glass and metal. Work that is domed or has edges is often rigid enough that counterenamel may not be needed.

Test Panels

There is little resemblance between enamel powders and the rich vibrant colors they reveal after firing. A universal fixture in every enameling studio is a collection of small copper panels that show the results of each enamel. While every enamelist will have a slightly different approach, the goal is always the same—to illustrate the potential of each enamel in a series of conditions.

For opaque enamels

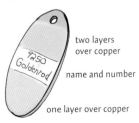

9250
Goldenrod

two layers over copper

name and number

one layer over copper

For transparent and translucent

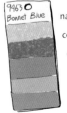

9463
Bonnet Blue

name and number

color over silver foil

color over gold foil

color over flux

color over opaque white

color over copper

Enameling

Champlevé

Champlevé (shomp-le-VAY) is perhaps the oldest
form of enameling. Metal is prepared with recesses
that are filled with enamel powder that is then
fused in place. Recesses can be of any size and
shape and may be made by engraving, chasing,
etching or other techniques.

Cloisonné

The word cloisonné (kloy-zo-NAY) is French and
means "partitioned area." Flat wires are bent to
shape and set on edge to create the compartments
into which enamel is fused.

Plique-á-jour

Plique-á-jour, French, derived from the words for "applied walls" and
"open to the light." One way to describe plique-á-
jour is to imagine carefully grinding away the back
of a champlevé or cloisonné panel until light could
pass through the glass. The effect is like a stained-
glass window.

Basse-taille

The French term basse-taille (bas-TY) means "low
cut." This technique is the similar to champlevé, but
the floor of the recess is patterned or ornamented.
This can be part of the recess-making step or a
second process altogether. For instance, recesses
could be created by piercing, then ornamented by engraving.

Grisaille

In this process, (griz EYE) the metal piece is first fired with a smooth,
even layer of a dark color, usually black. Extremely fine white enamel
(200 mesh) is mixed with water, turpentine,
and either oil of lavender or oil of clove to make
what we might call a silica-based paint. This is
applied with a brush using thick layers for light
areas and thinner layers to create shades of gray.
After thorough drying, the piece is fired the
same as other enamels.

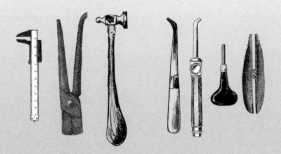

Chapter 4
Shaping

Sawing

Process

When done correctly, sawing is a relaxed and rhythmic experience. Muscles are loose and fluid, time seems to slow down and the saw propels itself. By contrast, when one factor is out of whack, the whole enterprise is frustrating.

> Hold the workpiece flat and steady on a stable bench pin.
> Be sure the blade is tightly strung in the sawframe.
> The teeth of the blade must point toward the handle.
> Saw with the blade vertical at a right angle to the workpiece.
> Keep the hand that holds the sawframe relaxed.

Blade Insertion

METHOD ONE

Clamp one end of the blade in place and tighten the screw finger-tight. Lean the frame against the bench, blade uppermost, and press hard enough to collapse the frame. Slide the loose end of the blade into place and tighten the screw. When you release tension, the frame will spring back and tighten the blade.

METHOD TWO

Set the blade into position, being sure the teeth point outward and toward the handle. Tighten the gripping plates at each end of the blade then use both hands to slide the frame open. Hold your thumb on the back of the frame and tighten the screw to lock the frame into position.

Blade Size

Ideally there will be three teeth on the metal at all times. Slight differences are okay, but if you are way off, the blade will be difficult to control and more likely to break. Here are some guidelines:

22–24 ga.	3/0 or similar
16–20 ga.	1/0 or similar
10–18 ga.	1 or similar

Piercing

Begin by drilling a hole in each compartment to be sawn. With the blade secured into the frame at one end, thread the other end of the blade through the hole and connect to the frame as usual. After the cut is complete, refine the shape by filing with the blade, rubbing it along the sawn edge.

Filing & Scoring

Files

It's easy to think of a
file as a simple tool that
rounds off sharp edges, but in skilled hands, files can do much more.
Skill consists of using the correct file, proper stroke, and stable grip.
See the Tools chapter for information on the files themselves.

Stroke

All files cut on the push stroke,
away from the handle. Files
cut in proportion to the force
behind them. Place your index
finger on the top face of the file
to improve control and increase
leverage. A downward force
is only as good as the upward
support beneath it, which is why
the bench pin is so important.
To extend the life of the tool, lift
up slightly on the return pass.

Sweeps

Filings of
precious metals
are caught so
they can be sent
to a refiner or
remelted in the studio.
Traditionally, leather aprons
were attached to the underside
of the bench, a system that
guarantees almost total capture.
More common now is the
watchmaker's variation, in which
a drawer is pulled out to catch
filings as needed.

Scoring a Narrow Band

Use a square to scribe a perpendicular line, then file a notch on
the edge with a triangular file.
Repeat this file stroke, tilting the
workpiece a few degrees further
with each pass. Turn the workpiece around and repeat the process from the other side. Switch
to a square needle file and refine
the groove to a uniform depth.
Bend with fingers, check against
a square, flux, and solder.

Scoring a Wide Panel

Use a square against this edge
to scribe a clear line. Clamp the
metal onto a workbench with
C-clamps and protective pads,
and at the same time, clamp a
straight piece of wood or steel
beside the marked line to guide
the tool. Set a sharp scoring
tool against the fence and pull it
firmly toward yourself. Continue
until a raised line is visible on
the reverse side of the sheet.

Forging

Forging

Forging is the controlled shaping of metal by the force of a hammer. This technique lends itself to graceful transitions from plane to plane and appealing contrasts of thick and thin sections. In good forging there is very little filing. Force and control must work together.

Control

Control in forging comes from the cross peen. Its wedge shape can push the metal in only two directions.

This push can be directed along the axis to increase length or outward from the axis to increase breadth.

Forging a Taper

Strike a series of blows along each side of a square rod, starting first at the top of the intended taper (1), then a second series, starting further down (2). Repeat as much as necessary to complete the taper. Planish out bumps by rotating.

Tips

> Sit or stand close to the work in a posture you can comfortably maintain.

> Work on a smooth, hard, stable surface.

> Keep your fingers and thumb wrapped around the hammer handle, not pointing along it.

> Anneal as needed: don't press your luck.

> Keep the hammer face polished.

> The hammer must make solid contact with the anvil; don't strike with a "jelly wrist."

> Don't hold the workpiece where you intend to hit it.

Double-sided forging

Most people forge on the flat face of an anvil, but an alternative method uses the curve of an anvil horn or stake to force the metal to flow outward from the point of contact.

Rhombus

This lopsided square cross section shape is easy to make but hard to correct. Continued striking will only make the problem worse, so correct these as soon as you see them form. File off the red areas, or forge the piece into a round rod and from there, return to a square section.

Drawing Wires & Tubes

Drawing Wire
Historians cannot be sure exactly when drawplates were invented, but they were in use in Europe in the 13th century. Drawplates are used to reduce the diameter of wires, to change cross sections, to make tubing, to smooth chains and to harden wire.

Process

1. Clamp the plate horizontally in a vise.
2. File a gradual taper at the tip of the wire.
3. Feed the tip of the wire through the unnumbered side of the plate into the first hole where it fits snugly. Use heavy-duty gripping pliers called draw tongs to pull the wire through the plate.
4. Pull the wire through successive holes until it feels tough and springy. Anneal and dry, then continue drawing.

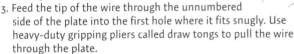

About those numbers...
The numbers on a drawplate have no correspondence to wire size. The largest hole on any drawplate is labeled #1 regardless of its diameter. A few manufacturers offer drawplates with holes in B&S sizes.

Cross section
Drawplates are made in a variety of cross section shapes such as triangular, star-shaped, and oval. These are somewhat rare and have limited use because the shapes are so specific.

Making a Tube
1. Cut a strip of thin gauge metal with parallel sides; cut a point on the strip.

2. Lay the annealed strip in a groove cut into endgrain or a V-block. Set a rod along the center line and strike it with a mallet.

3. Continue bending this trough into a tube. Take special care that the point is symmetrically formed.

4. Pull the strip through the drawplate just like wire. Continue pulling until the edges just meet—do not overlap the seam.

5. Solder the seam, usually with hard solder. Prop it up on a brick so the seam remains upright and easy to watch during soldering.

Shallow Forming

General Rules

> Use your fingers as much as possible. Wood, plastic, or rawhide tools are used next, and steel tools (hammers, pliers, etc.) only when absolutely required.

> Whenever possible, anneal the metal. This step takes less time than removing the marks that can result from working on unyielding material.

Dapping

Dapping uses a die and punches to create domes from disks of sheet metal.

Dapping dies are made in steel, brass, and wood, usually in the form of a cube with depressions on each side. Dapping punches are short, steel rods with a symmetrical dome or sphere on one end.

1. Cut out and anneal a disk.
2. Select a die cup that is a little larger than the disk, and a punch that makes a loose fit in it.
3. Drop the disk into the cup and strike a few light blows. Stop when the punch makes solid contact in the cup.
4. Transfer the dome to a smaller die cup and strike it again with the appropriate punch.

Shallow Forming

Shallow forming (also called "bossing") is a method of giving minor curves to sheet metal. It usually

makes a piece look thicker and, because curved surfaces show more reflections than flat sheets, the result appears brighter. Bossed areas are structurally rigid.

1. Saw out the shape.
2. After annealing, work the metal on a yielding surface with a mallet, hammer, or punch.
3. To blend the edges into the piece, form them over a dapping punch or hammer held in a vise.

Working Surfaces

pitch

soft wood

micro-crystalline wax

leather

Repoussé

Repoussé

Repoussé is one of the oldest metalsmithing techniques in the world. Virtually every ancient culture with a tradition of metalwork has left examples of this technique. The word comes from the French verb meaning "to push back." Simply stated, repoussé is the process of creating volumetric forms by pushing metal.

Tools for Repoussé

Although tools can be bought, many people prefer to make their own. Only a few are needed to begin, but a collection of 40 or 50 is typical. Tools are usually hardened and tempered.

Tracers, for making lines

Modeling & planishing

Curved punches

Matting tools

Process

1. Draw the design on annealed metal.

2. Warm the pitch with a gentle flame and set the metal right-side up onto a smooth area of pitch. Pull a rim of pitch onto the metal to achieve a better grip.

3. Go over the lines lightly with a tracing punch.

4. Lift the metal out of the pitch by warming it and lifting with tweezers. Remove excess pitch by burning or (better) by dissolving it in baby oil or turpentine.

5. Turn the metal over and set it back into the pitch. Boss up forms with whatever round-tipped tools will fit the shapes. When the metal feels stiff, remove it, clean off the pitch and anneal.

6. Dry the sheet and return it to the pitch for further work on either side as needed.

Sinking

Sinking

Sinking is a versatile technique used to create domed forms in sheet metal by pounding the metal into a hemispherical die. Sinking can be used by itself or as a first step in raising.

Process

1. Scribe a circle with dividers and cut out a disk. Thickness for small vessels is 18 or 20 gauge.

2. Draw pencil guidelines with a compass on the inside of the form at ½" intervals.

3. Place the disk so the edge crosses the center of a depression carved into a stump or wood block. Strike with a ball-faced hammer or mallet, progressing from the circumference in toward the center.

4. Anneal as needed. When the desired depth has been reached, smooth the form over a mushroom stake.

Tools

Sinking blocks are usually made of wood, preferably using the end grain. Carve depressions with gouges or turn them on a lathe. The die shapes are general forming aids and do not need to exactly fit the final shape. Mallets are generally preferred over hammers because they cause less stress on the workpiece, but the added weight of steel hammers has the advantage of speeding up the process.

Seaming

Seaming

Although any shape can be raised from a flat sheet, it is sometimes more efficient to fabricate a shape that approaches the desired end result and use forming techniques from there. The solder seams in such pieces will receive a lot of stress so some special provisions must be made.

Interlocking Finger Joint

1. File or planish a bevel equal to about five thicknesses of the metal. Angle the two ends of the strip in opposite directions so when they connect they will mate to make a smooth joint.

2. To prevent the two edges from sliding past each other, cut and bend tabs in each end. Mark a line ¼" in from each edge and lay out the same number of tabs on each edge. Generally, the tabs are of equal size, but variations are possible.

3. Saw these lines on both sides, stopping at the ¼" mark. On stock under 20 gauge a single cut is sufficient, but for heavier sheet, cut a skinny V.

4. On one edge, bend the even-numbered tabs up slightly. On the other edge bend the even-numbered tabs down. Paint the whole area with flux, slide the edges together, and wrap with binding wire.

5. Set the form over a stake and mallet the tabs down.

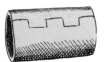

6. Apply solder generously—there is more surface area here than meets the eye. After soldering, quench in water and examine the joint. If there are voids, planish the seam, reflux, and remelt the solder.

Raising

There is only one right way to raise—the way that works. Methods will differ depending on the size and shape of the piece, the tools available, and the metal being raised.

1. Centerpunch the sheet and scribe a circle with dividers. Cut with shears, then file and burnish the edge to make it smooth.

2. Draw concentric guidelines about ¼" apart with a pencil compass. Give the sheet contour by sinking or angle raising.

3. Because material at the edge has to cover a greater distance than the metal near the base line, raise a course or two starting at mid-height.

4. To begin raising, hold the form at about a 30° angle, and strike the hammer so its leading edge touches the metal first. The idea is to compress the metal, pushing it into itself.

5. As work proceeds, rotate the disk and drop the hammer in even blows. After going around the form once, slide the disk back about ½" and continue raising.

6. The idea is to make a bulge and then work it to the edge. As you work, experiment with the angle of the work against the stake to find the most efficient position.

7. As raising continues, the top edge will thicken slightly. To exaggerate this, tap the edge with a cross peen at the end of each course. Support the work on a sandbag or in your hand while doing this.

8. Check the straightness of the form with a surface gauge or by drawing lines with a stationary pencil. Cut the top as needed and file it smooth. Planish as described on the next page.

Raising

Planishing

This word comes from the Latin *planus*, which means to flatten or level. It refers to the smoothing, toughening, and polishing of metal by hammering. Hammer faces and stakes or anvil must be mirror-finished.

A hammer held in a vise can be used like a stake.

... and so can a dapping punch held in a vise.

Disk Size

The diameter of the starting disk is the sum of the widest and tallest measures (AB + CD) or, for a dome, twice the length of line AB.

Raising Stake

You can make your own raising stake from a piece of hardwood, or even a common two-by-four. A valley in one end is used for crimping, and the rounded tip of the other stands in for a T-stake.

18"

Hammers

Any smooth-faced hammer can be used for planishing but the ideal tool has one flat face and one slightly crowned face. A heavy hammer (12–16 oz.) is best for quick work and flattening wire, but a lightweight hammer (3–6 oz.) is recommended for final finishing.

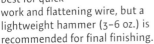

Mallets

Raising with mallets goes slower than with hammers, but the time might be saved because less planishing is needed. Use wood, horn, nylon, delrin, or other plastics.

Anticlastic Raising

Terminology

The word synclastic describes a form in which the dominant curves both move in the same direction. When the two dominant axes curve in opposite directions, the result is known as an anticlastic form. A bowl is a synclastic form and a saddle is an anticlastic form.

Sinusoidal Stakes

A flat sinusoidal stake can be made of hardwood or plastic. A metal variety is made by bending a tapered steel rod. All curves should be smooth, uniform, and symmetrical.

1. Cut a graceful form and file the edges smooth. Shapes do not need to be symmetrical but this is recommended in early learning exercises. Trace the pattern for future reference.

2. Bend the annealed sheet into an even curve and lay it over the stake. While holding the legs together, strike the metal with a smooth cross-peen hammer or mallet to begin the curve.

3. Move along the edge, starting in the center and moving outward, left and right. Reverse the metal and repeat on the opposite edge.

4. Continue on the long axis to gradually roll the form upward. Use gentle overlapping blows, stopping as needed to manually twist the piece back to symmetry.

5. Stop when the form is oval in cross section. Anneal and dry. Hold the form beside a curved stake like an anvil horn or a ring mandrel gripped in a vise. Tap on the edge directly opposite from the point of contact, rolling the form and advancing along that point.

Die Forming

Categories of Die Forming

Non-conforming punch dies

Non-conforming silhouette dies

Embossing dies

Conforming punch dies

Cutting (blanking) dies

Combination
  (e.g., silhouette with detail)

Uses

Die forming has many applications but is especially good for:

* matching halves, like spouts or
  a box and lid
* production situations with interchangeable parts
* designs with repeated elements

Silhouette Dies

Silhouette dies have an outline
(silhouette) of a desired shape cut
in a rigid material (the die). Metal is
pushed into the open area. Variations
involve the die material, the ram, the
force behind the ram, and the method
of holding the workpiece to the die.

*Silhouette dies allow a variety of
depths to be made in a single die.*

Wooden Dies

1. Make a die block by gluing together pieces of
   plywood and tempered Masonite.

2. If you use a band saw instead of a coping saw,
   close the opening by gluing in a strip of wood.

3. Make a rubbing of the die and use this to cut
   the metal and locate the holes for screws.
   The holes should be a little larger than the
   threaded part of the screws.

4. Fasten the metal onto the die with ¾" sheet
   metal screws. To reveal the outline of the form,
   tap the metal lightly with a mallet. While
   working, the die can sit on a bench, sandbag, or
   opened vise. To anneal the workpiece, remove
   the screws and take the metal off the die.

Die Forming

Hydraulic Forming

A hydraulic jack uses fluid to exaggerate a movement of one piston into a greater movement of another piston. Such a jack can be positioned in a stable frame so that the pushing action of its ram is trapped behind a fixed plate. This is called a hydraulic press; when it is used to form metal in a die, the process is called hydraulic die forming.

Equipment

Presses are available in several sizes and with jacks of varying pressure. Press frames are simple in concept and exacting in practice. Joints must be strong and alignment precise or the frame can literally tear itself apart. Buy a well-engineered and well-built tool from the beginning.

Containing the Action

A simple version of a press die would have a punch coming down on a sheet of annealed metal as it rests on a rubbery pad. In this configuration a lot of the "give" of the pad is dispersed outward which wastes the force of the ram. To eliminate this wasted energy, the yielding pad is fitted into a steel box or cylinder.

Urethane

In ancient times, lead was used to force thin sheet metal into bronze dies. A modern synthetic material called urethane is preferred today because it is safer and more efficient. Urethane can be manufactured to include a variety of properties, including a wide range of hardness, known as Shore Hardness. Because it is measured with a tool called a durometer, this term is also used. Urethanes run from 20 durometers (pencil eraser soft) to 95 durometers (used for car bumpers). Urethanes are impervious to water, oil, and oxidation but will start to break down at temperatures above 250° F (121° C). Never heat, burn, saw, or sand urethane because dangerous gases are released. Always cut with scissors or a knife.

Metal Clay

Concept

An organic binder provides elasticity while holding very tiny grains of metal in suspension. After drying, an object is heated, which causes the binding material to burn away and the particles to fuse. This water-soluble product is available from several manufacturers in the form of lump, sheets, slip, and ready-to-use syringes.

The process is easiest with pure silver and pure gold because these noble metals resist the formation of oxides and fuse at easily attainable temperatures.

Working with Metal Clay

The working properties of metal clays are related to moisture content. Avoid working in a draft or using materials that will absorb water (like paper and cardboard). Take only the amount to be used at the moment, sealing the rest in plastic wrap to keep it moist.

To make sheets of metal clay, roll it out like cookie dough, using a convenient length of plastic pipe as a rolling pin. To ensure uniform thickness, set matching spacers on each side of the clay. Tongue depressors, pieces of mat board or stacks of playing cards make good spacers.

Cut metal clay by dragging a needle through the material or with a knife, (which leaves a neater edge). A long, razorlike medical industry tool called a tissue blade is a useful (though dangerous) cutting tool. Plastic picnic knives make a nice alternative when children are involved, and the edge of a playing card works too.

Patterned Rollers

Carve a pattern into a length of PVC pipe with linoleum cutters, wood carving tools, or gravers. If a specific repeat length is desired, use a cylinder with a diameter of one-third the intended repeat. A mark on a 1" pipe will reappear about every three inches when rolled.

Textures

Metal clays are great at capturing textures—simply press the metal clay against an object. To make a texture plate, carve into linoleum or polymer clay.

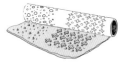

Metal Clay

Firing Equipment

The ideal tool for firing is an electric programmable kiln. These kilns combine the benefits of accurate control with freedom since they do not require monitoring. Several kilns have been developed just for metal clay and can be purchased through jewelry supply companies.

Next best is a manual kiln with an accurate pyrometer. As the kiln approaches the desired temperature, regulate the heat by adjusting the knob or cracking the door open. Kilns appropriate for this method include enameling kilns, burnout ovens, test (glaze) kilns, and kilns used to fuse or anneal glass. Large ceramic kilns are not recommended because the internal temperature varies throughout the chamber.

Some metal clays have been created to have relatively short firing times. These open the possibility of alternate firing techniques using a torch, camp stove, or alcohol-based fuel. Because technology is changing rapidly, consult the web or contact a supplier of metal clay for the latest information.

Firing with a Torch

Some versions of metal clay are made of such tiny particles that they can be fused quickly enough to make torch firing practical. A few minutes at a glowing red color is enough to make the metal solid. Simply set the dried object on a soldering or firing surface and heat it evenly with a torch.

An alternate approach is to jerryrig a furnace from a flower pot. Line the terra cotta pot with aluminum foil to reflect the heat, and find a way to prop a jeweler's torch so that its flame is directed into the chamber. This method reaches around 1500° F (815° C), which is good for several versions of metal clay. It is practical for 10-minute firings; something that isn't comfortable when you're holding the torch the whole time.

Laboratory-Grown Gems

Lab-grown gems can withstand the firing temperatures of metal clay. Press into place and fire as usual. Allow to air cool. These stones will be clearly identified as "lab-grown" by reputable vendors.

Finishing

After firing, metal clays are 100% metal and can be soldered, filed, sanded, oxidized, patinaed and polished like any other metal. Because of their porous nature, high-shrinkage materials like original PMC should be burnished or tumbled to compact the structure before finishing.

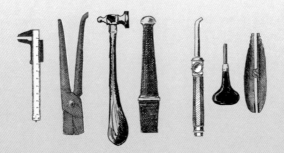

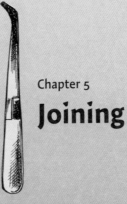

Chapter 5
Joining

Rivets

Basic Rivets

Rivets are ancient, universal and brilliant examples of a mechanical joint. A metal pin is fed through holes in the parts to be joined, then a projecting tip on each end is hammered back on itself to create a head that locks the stack together. Rivets are used to hold steel girders together, to grip handles to knives, and in a thousand other uses from aircraft to xylophones.

Process

1. Select a drill and wire of the same size. If you don't have a perfect match, start with a larger wire and sand a gradual taper.
2. Drill all the holes you need in one piece; drill one hole in the other piece.
3. Insert the wire, snip and file so a tip equal to roughly half the thickness of the wire extends on both sides.
4. Set the work on a solid surface, suspended so that the wire still sticks out of both sides. Strike the end lightly with a sharp cross-peen hammer.
5. Flip the piece over and repeat; continue as needed until heads form on both ends of the wire.
6. Drill another hole and repeat. When two rivets are in place, drill and set all the remaining rivets.

Nailhead Rivets

This popular version of rivets is useful when a larger head is needed, either for the look of it or because the material being held requires a wider grip. It is also handy when one end of the rivet is difficult to reach, for instance, inside a cup.

1. Draw a bead on a wire with a hot, sharp flame point.

2. Slide the wire into a tight hole on the numbered side of the drawplate. Strike with a planishing hammer to flatten the bead.

3. Shape the resulting nailhead with punches or a nail set while still in the drawplate, or remove it and file to a desired shape.

4. Slide the wire into the workpiece, trim to the correct length and form a standard rivet head on the other end.

Special Rivets

Tube Rivets
These gentle rivets are recommended when hammering might cause damage. This would include enamels, delicate mechanisms and stones.

1. As with other rivets, the first step is to drill a hole through all the pieces being joined. This must make a tight fit with the chosen tube.

2. Slide the tube into position and saw it so no more than half a diameter is sticking out on each side. The tube seam should be soldered and the tube annealed.

3. Set a scribe into the tube and swing it around to flare out the mouth. Repeat this on the other end of the tube.

4. Set the rivet on a round punch and tap it with another round punch to curl the edges outward.

Flush Rivets
Start by making holes that match the wire size. Bevel the upper edge of each hole so that the swell of the rivet will be below the surface of the materials being joined. Either or both ends of a rivet can be made flush. If the rivet is made of the same metal as the piece it is holding, the rivet will blend in completely. After forming the rivet head, planish, file, sand, and polish.

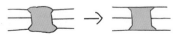

Cutlers Rivets
This ingenious mechanical closure works because of friction between its parts, all taking place inside a tube.

> The solid rod should be slightly larger than the interior of the tube. Only slightly.
> File a chamfer on the solid rod to help it track into the tube.
> The hole in the material being joined must be a bit larger than the tube because it will swell as the parts are engaged.
> Use a vise or C-clamp to apply even pressure as the parts are squeezed together.

More Cold Connections

Tabs

Tabs provide a simple and secure cold connection by bending a finger of metal on one piece over another piece. Bending is usually begun with pliers and finished with a mallet. Finishing is typically done before the pieces are joined.

Variations

Tabs can reach from inside a pierced form.

Use tabs with steps to create space between layers.

Tabs can take interesting shapes.

Threaded Elements

Because screws, bolts, and jar lids are ubiquitous in modern life, we can easily forget their magic. The two most common systems in the US are called National Coarse (N/C) and National Fine (N/F). Sizes are identified by two numbers, the first referring to diameter (or in small screws, a number from 2–12) followed by the counted threads per inch. The tool that cuts an interior thread is called a tap and looks like a tapered screw with several channels cut along its long axis. Threading dies are used to cut threads on the outside of a rod or cylinder, and usually take the form of a thick steel disk with four holes in the center. Both tools are made with a specific size and pitch, which means that you must use a matching set.

Tapping a Hole

1. Drill a hole of the correct size—this is important. Hold the tap so it is perpendicular to the work, and screw it in until it bites into the metal. Add light lubrication and screw it half a turn further. Reverse the action, unscrewing enough to clear the cuttings from the tap. Screw and reverse, continuing this rhythm until the tap rotates easily.

Using a Threading Die

The diameter of the starting rod should be equal to the finished outside diameter of the threads. Screw the die onto the tapered end slowly. Rotate a full turn, then unscrew a half turn to clear away the chips that were just cut. Continue in this way—full turn forward, half turn back—until the die spins easily. Add a few drops of light oil every few turns to lubricate and wash away the chips.

Torches

Torch Safety

> Secure tanks so they cannot tip over, for instance by chaining them to a table leg.

> Use only correct fittings. Never modify a fitting or use tape to enhance a joint. If the threads are not sufficient to prevent leaks, return the tank and fitting to a dealer immediately.

> Check each junction with soapy water every time the tank is changed.

> Never allow grease or oil to come in contact with oxygen.

> Do not use excessive force when tightening fittings or when turning off a torch. This can impair the fit.

> Get in the habit of sniffing the air before soldering. If there is a trace of fuel smell, open a window, disconnect the torch, set it safely outside and call a supplier to come and pick it up.

Flame Types

Reducing - Bushy, pulsing flame, deep blue color. This fuel-rich flame absorbs oxides.

Neutral - Sharp point, gentle hiss, medium blue color. All the fuel gas is being burned. The hottest point is ¾" in front of the cone.

Oxidizing - Thin cone, angry hiss, pale lavender color.

Types of Torches

> **fuel / atmosphere**
(a.k.a Presto-Lite)
The flow of the fuel draws air into the torch.

> **fuel / forced air**
A blowpipe, bellows, or compressor provides atmospheric air.

> **fuel / oxygen**
Pure oxygen (five times richer than atmospheric air) is combined with fuel in the torch.

Flux

Flux

Fluxes work by forming a coating that protects metal from oxidation. When heated, the water evaporates leaving a clear glassy coating that is more attractive to oxygen than the metal being soldered. As flux absorbes oxygen, its protective power diminishes.

Borax

This is probably the most commonly used flux worldwide, though it is less common in the US. Borax melts at 167° F (75° C).

Cupronil

This is a commercial flux similar to Prips but especially good at preserving a finish through a heating operation.

Handy Flux

A borax-based compound provides substantial oxide protection and leaves a tough glassy skin. The flux becomes clear and fluid at 1100° F (600° C) and is effective up to 1600° F, (870°C).

Battern's (My-T-Flux, etc.)

A yellow or green, fluoride-based flux with a watery consistency. It is called self-pickling because it doesn't leave a resilient flux glass like boron-based fluxes.

Prip's Flux

Borax	75 ml
Boric Acid	90 ml
Tri-Sodium Phosphate (TSP)	75 ml

Boil these ingredients in two quarts of water until dissolved.

This flux is a popular protection against firescale. To build a thick glassy coat, warm the work slightly, and quench it in Prip's solution. Repeat several times. An alternative is to warm the work then spritz solution from a spray jar. Again, several applications are recommended. The resulting glassy skin is waterproof, so it can be sustained throughout several solderings if you quench only in water. It will dissolve in pickle.

Boric Acid & Alcohol

This is a time-honored way to protect against oxidation and firescale. To make the solution, add boric acid to denatured alcohol until it stops dissolving (i.e., make a saturated solution). The resulting thin paste will need to be shaken or stirred periodically. To use it, dip the work into the solution, set it on a soldering block and ignite it. The alcohol will quickly burn off, leaving a white film of borax. Many jewelers paint a little Handy Flux on the joint in conjunction with this. This is a highly flammable liquid and must be used carefully. For safety's sake, keep only a small jar on the soldering bench.

Pickle

Pickle

Pickle is a chemical bath used to dissolve surface oxidation and flux residue from a metal surface. Pickles work at room temperature but the reaction is hastened with heat.

Sparex

Sparex (sodium bisulfate) works best at about 180° F (80° C). It should never be heated to a boil because 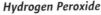 dangerous fumes will be generated. A convenient vessel is a crock pot that has had its seams sealed with tub caulk. As a substitute for jewelers' pickle, use a swimming pool additive intended to lower the pH of the water—it has the same active ingredient as Sparex.

Hydrogen Peroxide

Normal pickle will remove some oxides from brass, but usually leaves a rosy-colored copper layer. To remove it, first clean the work in warm standard Sparex. Mix a tablespoon of Sparex crystals into a cup of hydrogen peroxide (H_2O_2 available at drugstores). Quantities may be multiplied as needed for larger scale work.

Warm the piece slightly and dip it into the peroxide solution. Repeat as necessary to remove the pink layer. The peroxide solution will give up its extra oxygen atom to the air, so it is only active for a short time. Mix fresh solution as needed. If brass is left in the solution overnight, it can be damaged by etching.

When Good Pickle Goes Bad

Pickle absorbs oxides like a sponge soaks up a spill and, like a sponge, pickle will reach a point where it has taken on about all it can carry. The first indication that pickle is reaching saturation is that it will become blue, but even at a bright blue the pickle has some life left. When it takes longer than a couple minutes to dissolve oxides, it is time to replace the solution.

Before discarding, neutralize the pickle by adding baking soda. The solution will froth up, so work in a sink. When the bubbling reaction slows down it is safe to flush the solution down the pipes.

Soldering & Fusing

Fusing

Fusing is the process of heating pieces of metal to their melting point and allowing the puddled surfaces to flow together. This technique has limited control, but can create rich textures and unusual effects. Metals that are good heat conductors (like silver and gold) fuse well, but because it is difficult to localize the heat, fusion is not practical for precise work. Coat the metal pieces with flux and heat them so that they all reach the melting point simultaneously.

Soldering

At soldering temperatures, the crystals of metal move apart, opening up microscopic spaces. The idea behind soldering is to introduce an alloy that is fluid exactly at the point of maximum expansion. This alloy, (solder), flows into the spaces to create an intercrystalline bond.

| *tight fit* | *crystals expand* | *solder (red) enters by capillary action* | *solder is diffused into the structure* |

Common Soldering Problems

PROBLEM	REASON	SOLUTION
Incomplete or unsoldered joint	Not enough heat; metal was dirty; no flux; prolonged heating.	Avoid playing the flame directly on the solder.
Solder balls up	Metal or solder may be dirty.	Reflux and try again.
Solder jumps to one side of joint	One side is hotter than the other.	Keep the torch moving so all parts heat equally.
Solder spills out into a large puddle	Too much solder; too high a heat.	Use smaller pieces of solder; level the heat as you approach the flow temperature.

Soldering Methods

Rules for Soldering

— The pieces must make a tight fit.

— The joint and solder must be clean: no grease, pickle, buffing compound, etc.

— Use flux to protect the metal from oxidation. Each reheating usually requires refluxing.

— All the pieces being soldered should reach soldering temperature simultaneously. Heat the adjacent areas to reduce the flow of heat away from the joint. Take into account heat sinks such as binding wire, steel mesh, and locking tweezers.

— When possible, position the torch so as to draw solder through a joint. Generally, avoid directing the flame at solder.

— Use just enough solder to fill the joint.

— When soldering an enclosed area, provide an escape for the steam trapped inside. If not vented, this will expand and can cause the piece to explode.

— Metal temperatures are judged by color changes which can be seen best in a dimly lit area. Whatever your lighting, keep it consistent.

Soldering Methods

Chip (paillon)
• Probably the most commonly used method.
• Puts the correct amount of solder at the right place.
• The solder itself serves as temperature indicator.

Sweat (tinning)
• Keeps solder out of sight when doing overlay.
• Provides more control when soldering large and small pieces together.
• Helps direct solder flow.

Pick (probe)
• Especially good when the configuration of work makes placement of solder difficult.
• An efficient method.
• Good for production work.

Wire (stick)
• This has the advantages of the probe method and eliminates cutting the solder.
• Good heat control is important or excess solder is used.

Mud (paste)
• Commonly used in commercial assembly line soldering.
• Good for delicate work such as filigree.

Firescale

Firescale

The Jeweler's Bane, firescale is an insidious deposit of cupric oxide that grows within the structure of some copper alloys such as sterling and low karat gold. It is also called Fire Coat, Fire Mark, and Fire Stain.

What Happens

When copper-bearing alloys are heated in the presence of oxygen, oxides are quickly formed. Cuprous oxide (CuO) is a black surface layer that can usually be dissolved in pickle. Cupric oxide (Cu_2O) is a purplish compound that forms simultaneously within the metal. This is firescale.

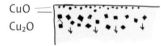
CuO
Cu_2O

Prevention

> Avoid prolonged heating—use a "hit and run" soldering technique.

> Use a big enough flame to get the job done efficiently. A small flame can cause, not prevent, firescale because it extends the soldering time.

> Use enough flux. Flux absorbs oxygen and prevents it from combining with copper.

> Do not overheat when soldering. Silver and gold alloys should never need to go above a medium red when soldering.

Depletion Gilding

In the studio, a process called depletion gilding can be used on sterling and karat golds to create a layer of oxide-free metal over an object to cover scale. Copper in the alloy is converted to copper oxide by heating, and this is then selectively removed in pickle. In essence, the alloys are broken apart, leaving a thin coating of pure silver or gold on the surface.

After all soldering and finishing is complete (but before patination or stonesetting), heat the work until a gray oxide forms, then quench it in clean pickle. Repeat the procedure 3 to 5 times, rinsing in water and lightly scratchbrushing each time. Remember to protect yourself against splashing pickle.

Bright Dipping

Firescale can be removed by dipping work in a strong solution of nitric acid and water. After all soldering and rough finishing are done (but before stones are set), attach the piece to a wire and dunk it for only a few seconds into a 50/50 solution at room temperature. Firescale will turn dark gray. Rinse and scratchbrush. Repeat until the scale is gone. Wear rubber gloves and protective clothing.

Problem Solving

Problem   My rivets always seem to bend over instead of making a nice-looking dome on the end.

Reason   You're leaving too much of the rivet wire standing up above the surface.

Solution   Snip then file the end of the rivet wire so that the wire projecting above the surface equals no more than half its diameter.

Problem   The solder won't flow, even though the metal is glowing red.

Reason   No flux, or the flux has become saturated and is not doing its job. Or, oils, dirt, paint, graphite, etc. on the metal.

Solution   Clean the metal well, either in pickle or with abrasives like Scotch-Brite, sandpaper, or sandblasting. Apply fresh flux and solder and try again. By the way, there's no reason to get to a bright glowing red. Slow down, Tiger.

Problem   The solder balls up.

Reason   Tarnish (oxide) on the solder, either before you started, or created as you worked.

Solution   Always scrub solder with Scotch-Brite before cutting it, or with wire, before each use. Once you've started soldering, don't take the torch flame off the metal. This invites oxygen to rush in where it will create oxides.

Problem   Epoxy doesn't hold well for me.

Reason   It's critical that you have equal amounts of resin and hardener, and equally important that they are well mixed.

Solution   Spend at least a minute stirring the parts together. The surfaces to be joined must be clean of oils, dirt and soap. Also, it helps if the surfaces have a tooth, so if possible, scrub it with medium grit sandpaper.

Adhesives

Adhesives

Adhesives used as a substitute for properly made mechanical or soldered connections are generally considered a sign of poor craftsmanship. There are situations however, when adhesives are a legitimate and important technique of heatless connecting. There are countless glues with more being developed each year. Here is a summary of the basic categories.

Type	Advantages	Disadvantages
Hide glue (a.k.a rabbit glue)	Easy to make, especially if you kill and clean animals for food. Inexpensive, water resistant, quick drying	Hygroscopic (takes moisture from the air) which can weaken the joint. When it gets very dry this glue becomes brittle.
Casein	Low cost, ease of use, and broad application. Most are water resistant and can be easily thinned to allow them to penetrate porous materials.	Not entirely waterproof. Subject to mold.
Polymer (Elmer's, SOBO, Duco Cement, etc.)	Very strong, waterproof, some versions set rapidly.	Moderate strength, low resistance to heat.
Epoxies	Clear, very tough, waterproof.	Relatively expensive, must be thoroughly mixed, breaks down around 400° F (200° C).
Cyanoacrylate (Super Glue, Krazy Glue, etc.)	Hardens instantly when air is excluded; strong, clear, waterproof.	Not good on porous surfaces, hard to position work, relatively expensive.

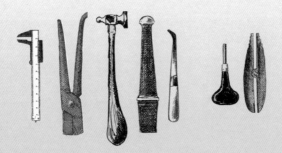

Chapter 6
Casting

Ingot Molds

Ingot Molds

Either buy a commercial ingot mold or make your own from sheet steel and square steel rod. Use small C-clamps to hold the mold together. File tiny air vents slanted upward along the mold so the air inside the mold can escape.

Using a Steel Ingot Mold

1. Lubricate the mold with soot, Vaseline, or mineral (baby) oil.
2. Heat the mold until the lubricant starts to smoke. Set the mold into a pan of sand or a cast-iron skillet to catch accidental spills.
3. Heat the metal in a pouring crucible, adding flux a couple of times. When making an alloy, start with the precious metals, then add the base metals.
4. Pour the metal through a reducing flame in a single even flow. Allow the red color to fade before removing the ingot from the mold. Quench in water.

Charcoal Molds

1. If the surface of the block is irregular, start by sanding it flat.
2. Carve a recess in a flat block of charcoal to the thickness and shape of the desired piece.
3. Melt the metal directly in the mold cavity. Flux is not usually needed because of the purifying atmosphere created by the charcoal.
4. When the metal is molten, bring a second charcoal block down on the first with even pressure. Work while standing to avoid an accident that would give new meaning to the term "lap dance." The mold can usually provide three or four castings.

Cuttlefish

Cuttlefish

For centuries goldsmiths have used cuttlefish skeletons as molds. This technique provides rich texture and immediate results at a low cost, and with very little equipment. A disadvantage of the process is that it is limited in size and thickness. Most cuttlefish are about 3" wide and 7" long.

Use two bones or cut one in half. Remove the pointy end.

2. Rub the pieces on coarse sandpaper or against each other (soft side to soft side) in a circular motion to make flat surfaces.

. Carve an indentation for the desired form. Remember that the depth of the cut equals the thickness of the final 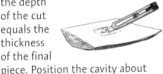 piece. Position the cavity about ¾" from the bigger end.

4. Carve a sprue funnel in both sides.

. Scratch vents upward to allow the escape of gases from inside the mold.

6. If you want to emphasize the grain pattern, stroke the cuttlefish with a soft dry brush. The material between the grain ridges is soft and will quickly fall away.

. Tie the mold halves together with binding wire or masking tape.

8. Set the mold into sand or pumice to hold it upright. Melt the metal in a pouring ladle and fill the mold in a smooth pour.

Sand Casting

Mold Frame

These two parts, called the cope and drag, are identical except that one piece has pins projecting from one side while the other has sockets that receive the pins.

Preparing Sand

Almost any sand can be used, but bear in mind that the finer the sand, the better the detail on the resulting casting. Sift the sand through a coarse sieve several times to remove debris. Sift it through a finer screen or cheesecloth to remove large grains. Mix baby oil, glycerin, or motor oil into the sand by repeated stirring. Avoid making the sand too wet. If you goof, you'll need to add dry sand, so keep some aside just in case. To test for proper consistency, squeeze a handful of sand into a ball. You should be able to break the lump cleanly in half without having it crumble to pieces.

Casting a Small, Flat or Thin Object

Set one half of the mold onto a flat surface and fill it with prepared sand. Pack it down firmly with a block of wood and scrape off the surplus.

Set the other mold frame on top of the first. Dust the packed sand with pounce, lay the model into position and dust again. Sprinkle sand over the model and pack it ,layer by layer, until the second frame is full. Carefully flip the assembled mold upside down.

Carefully separate the frames and remove the model with tweezers. Clear away stray grains of sand with a soft brush. Carve a funnel that extends to the edge of the frame.

Set the mold parts back together and pour molten metal into the mold using a pouring crucible.

Overview: Lost Wax Process

Lost Wax Process

When the metalsmiths of ancient cultures first developed this technique, they made models of beeswax and coated them with layers of clay reinforced with straw or linen. Most jewelry casting today uses a variation on the lost wax method developed in ancient times. This page provides a summary of the process, which is explained in more detail throughout this chapter.

1. A model is made of wax or another completely combustible material.

2. The model is mounted on a wax rod called a sprue.

3. The sprue is mounted onto a base and positioned within a steel cylinder called a flask.

4. A plaster-like material called investment is mixed to a creamy consistency. Steps are taken to ensure that this mix is free of air bubbles.

5. The smooth investment is gently poured over the prepared model as it stands in the center of the flask.

6. The investment is dried and then burned out in a kiln. This cures the mold and removes all traces of the model.

7. While the mold is still hot from the burnout, molten metal is poured or forced into the mold, where it assumes the shape of the original model.

8. After brief cooling, the mold is quenched in water. This breaks the mold and releases the casting.

Equipment & Supplies

Flasks - Stainless steel cylinders are used to contain the mold. These need to match rubber sprue bases, so many studios limit their flask selection to two or three sizes. To improvise a flask, cut both ends off a steel can. Check with a magnet because aluminum soda cans won't work. Even steel cans normally last for only a few uses.

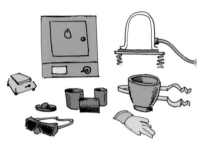

Sprue base - Buy rubber bases matched to your flasks; most studios can get along with fewer bases than flasks since they are only needed for about half an hour in the process. For irregular flasks (like cans), press clay onto a board or plastic lid.

Mixing bowl - Using a rubber dish cleans easily. Allow the investment to harden, then flex the bowl and the hardened investment will pop off. Alternatives: cottage cheese or deli containers.

Vacuum pump - This is used to remove bubbles from investment. While not essential for occasional casting, this device becomes important to consistently guarantee smooth castings and efficient cleanup. First choice: buy a small vacuum pump and mount it into a table. A smaller device called an aspirator uses the flow of tap water to draw a vacuum. These are available from suppliers of laboratory equipment.

Vibrator - This is an alternate way to remove bubbles. You can buy a small box-shaped vibrator made for this use or jury-rig an electric massager. Even cheaper, make an off-centered tool for a hand drill or flex shaft and use it to agitate the walls of the investment bowl.

Kiln - Any furnace that will safely reach 1300° F (700° C) will do. But the best kiln will be well insulated and will have a reliable pyrometer and a programming unit to control the rate and maximum temperature. New units use lightweight insulation instead of bricks but either will do the job. Coils and switches burn out with use but they are easy to replace. Contact the kiln manufacturer with the model number to be sure you get the correct replacement parts.

Tongs - For small-scale work, kitchen tongs can be substituted.

Gloves - Heat-resistant gloves are a good investment for casting studios, but in the meantime, work gloves offer some protection from heat.

Goggles - Sustained viewing of a torch flame is part of casting and can damage eyesight. Wear dark goggles—sunglasses are not sufficient.

Quench bucket - A plastic scrub bucket or joint compound container will do. It's useful to have two so you can trade off and allow one to settle out. The sludge is easier to discard when it is dry.

Hard Wax

Tools

> You can make carving tools from discarded dental tools, steel wire, bike spokes, coat hangers, or old silverware. Handles can be made from a dowel or a chopstick. You can also use a pin vise.

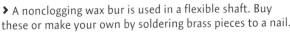

> A nonclogging wax bur is used in a flexible shaft. Buy these or make your own by soldering brass pieces to a nail.

> Coarse files (also called soft metal files), rasps, and utility knives are used to shape wax models.

> Use a spiral blade fitted in a standard sawframe to cut off sections of wax.

Building a Starting Block

For some forms, you can save time, effort, and expense by welding chunks of wax together. Heat blocks until both surfaces are gooey, then press the parts together and allow the wax to cool.

Lots of waste.

Scraps

Collect scrap pieces and keep them separate from metal, sawdust, and other debris. Put the scraps into a cardboard box lined with aluminum foil and heat slowly in an oven or kiln until they melt. Allow the block to cool slowly, then tear away the box.

Making Finger Holes

• Buy commercial wax tubes and cut off the width you need.
• Use a cylinder bur on a flex shaft to carve the blank from a block of wax.
• Warm a steel mandrel and slide the wax on, twisting slightly to prevent seizing.
• Use a mandrel with a blade attached.

Watch Your Weight

Because wax is lightweight, it is easy to make models too large. Final weight can be calculated by multiplying the weight of the wax by the specific gravity of the metal to be used. To reduce the weight of a model, carve out the inside with chisel points or a flex shaft bur.

Soft Wax & Organics

Working with Modeling Waxes

> Store wax sheets in a cool place, between pieces of paper, to keep them from sticking together.

> Before bending sheet wax, soften it by dipping it in warm water or breathing on it.

> Soft wax can be folded, twisted, stamped, pinched, pierced, built up, or pressed to receive a texture.

> All kinds of wax can be used together.

> A biology or clay needle makes a handy and inexpensive tool.

Cut with a utility blade. Transparency allows tracing.

Heat the needle at its center, not just the tip.

To add wax, touch a wire to a hot needle, and allow it to drop off the end.

Establishing a Ring Size

Wrap tape around a wooden dowel to make the correct size. To allow the wax pattern to slip off easier, lubricate the tape with Vaseline or oil.

Electric Wax Pen

These tools are preferred by professional wax workers because of their consistent temperature and ease of use. To make one, attach a light dimmer switch to a plug and connect a soldering iron.

Organic Models

Leaves, twigs, flower petals, and insects will burn out completely from an investment mold. This means they can be cast directly, often with very clear detail. Burnout usually takes longer for organic materials than for wax, and higher temperatures may also be needed.

Seal porous materials such as paper, cardboard, or popcorn by spraying, or painting with lacquer, wax, or thinned white glue. Spray delicate models like flower petals, or insect wings with several coats of fixative and reinforce thin sections by adding wax on the back.

Spruing

Sprues and Spruing

Sprues hold a model in its correct position while making the mold, provide a passageway for the escape of melting wax, and allow entry for molten metal.

> Arrange sprues to supply sufficient metal to each section of the model.
> Plan the location of sprues to avoid flowbacks and sharp curves.
> Attach sprues where they will cause the least damage to the model's surface texture and where they can be easily removed.
> Avoid spruing work dead level. Sprues should not enter at 90° angles.
> Sprue to the thickest section of the model. The sprue itself should be the thickest mass of the whole assembly.

Spruing	**NO**	**YES**	
Metal is expected to go through small passages to fill several larger areas.			Separate sprues are provided for each mass.
The metal is expected to flow back on itself.			This arrangement puts all the model downstream from the point of entry.
The sprue is attached to a thin section. This will cool first and stop further entrance of metal into the mold.			By attaching to the thickest section, porosity can be avoided.
The location of the sprue will damage the pattern.			Attaching the sprues to the edge of this ring will protect the surface pattern.

Porosity

If no extra material is supplied at the instant of contraction, metal will solidify with voids as it tries to fill the cavity. If the sprue and button are the last area to cool, porosity will occur here and no damage is done to the piece. To achieve this, set the thinnest (first cooling) area of the model furthest from the sprue base.

Investing

Investment

Modern investments are tough, more flexible, and less likely to separate in transit than mold materials of 20 years ago. Also, today's investments shrink less and can withstand faster ramping speeds. Platinum and palladium white gold require special investments because of their high melting temperatures.

Timing

Investments have 9–10 minutes of working time. If your pace is too slow, the investment will harden before it can coat the model. If you work too quickly and the investment is poured into the flask too soon, water in the mix is free to come out of solution creating raised streaks on the finished casting.

Hard Core Method

This is a time-tested method that is an alternative to vacuum investing. While this method is not quite as good at removing bubbles, it's possible to get very clean castings if you follow these steps carefully.

1. Mix investment and vibrate the bowl to remove bubbles.

2. Paint investment onto the model with a fine brush. Spread the mixture slowly to avoid trapping bubbles.

3. Sprinkle investment powder onto the coated model to absorb moisture and hasten the setting of this shell or core.

4. Set a flask over the model and pour in the investment. Keep weight off the model by pouring it down the side of the flask. Be sure to hold onto the base while pouring.

Burnout & Casting

Burnout

Burnout is usually done in a small electric kiln within 48 hours of investing. If burnout must wait, moisten the flask with water for a few seconds. The progression and pace of burnout will vary depending on the size and number of flasks in the kiln and the metal being cast. As a rule of thumb, allow two and a half hours for a typical burnout.

Temperatures (approximate)

°F	°C	
300	150	wax melts and drips out
450	235	wax ignites
600	325	woody materials ignite
1000	550	plastics vaporize
1250	650	wax residues vaporize
1350	740	gypsum binder breaks down, releasing sulfur that will cause oxidation. Do not go to this temperature.

Kiln Position

Place flasks in a kiln with the sprue holes facing down. Prop them to allow the wax to drip out.

Process

1. When burnout is complete, wind the machine, typically three rotations. Be sure you understand the locking mechanism before you begin. When complete, lock the arm in place.

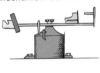

2. Put the charge of metal into the crucible. A tidy way to achieve this is to wrap the bits of metal in a tissue. Place the hot flask in the cradle of the casting machine.

3. Heat the metal until it is molten, adding flux a couple of times in the process. Direct the torch flame onto the lip of the crucible to prevent a cooling effect as the metal passes over this area.

4. Plant your feet firmly and grasp the arm of the casting machine. Pull back slightly to release the pin, then simultaneously let go of the arm and lift the torch a few inches. Resist the urge to scream and jump away. It makes people nervous.

Steam Casting

Surface Tension

The ingenious element of steam casting and sling casting is the way both methods remove the need for a crucible. Instead, metal is melted directly in the mouth of the sprue (a.k.a. the gate). Remember from school science when you saw water drip through a cloth, while honey wouldn't pass through the same cloth? The reason is the surface tension of the liquid, and this applies to molten metal too. For both these techniques, the trick is to make the sprues small enough that the surface tension of the metal prevents the metal from dripping in by gravity alone. This will be 16–gauge round wire, or strips that are no thicker than 16 gauge (1.29 mm) and no broader than ¾" (6.5 mm).

Process

1. If the sprue base did not form a large enough reservoir for melting, carve a funnel shape in the top of the invested flask. Use a knife and work over a wastebasket.
2. After standard burnout, remove the hot flask and set it on a heatproof surface (e.g., a brick) on a sturdy table, preferably no more than waist high.
3. Melt the metal in the mouth of the flask with a torch. Flux as usual.
4. When the metal is molten, withdraw the torch as you simultaneously clap the steam handle firmly onto the flask. Hold it in this position until the metal solidifies.
5. Allow the button to lose all redness, then quench in water. Avoid breathing the silica-laden steam.

Steam Casting Handle

Attach a jar lid to a comfortable handle. This can be a length of dowel, a file handle, a section of a tree branch or piece of wood. Use a screw for strength, and epoxy to prevent it from rotating. Line this with at least ¾" of newspaper or paper towels. Keep the tool in a bucket of water as you prepare the casting. When you're ready, lift the handle and allow excess water to drip off. The paper should be completely saturated but not dripping.

Simple Molds

Reusable Molds

In lost wax casting the investment mold must be destroyed to retrieve the finished casting (hence, "lost"). To make multiples, a supplementary step is needed to produce multiple wax models. These are made by injecting molten wax into a rubber mold that will flex sufficiently to allow the model to be removed.

Putty

A relatively new product is a two-part silicone-based material with the consistency of Silly Putty. The two component parts are of different colors, so blending is foolproof. Knead equal parts together until the color is uniform. Press the putty over an object, and allow it to sit until a fingernail poked into the rubber fails to leave a mark.

Alginate

Alginate is a short-life mold material that might be familiar to people who were fitted for dental braces. It is a water-soluble material made (delightfully enough) from seaweed. Mix with water to the consistency of mashed potatoes and press it onto the shape or texture you are duplicating. The mold will set up relatively quickly (5–10 minutes) and can be used right away. Alginate molds will dry and contract within 24 hours. To extend the life for a day or two, keep the mold in a dish of water.

Room Temperature Vulcanzing (RTV)

This two-part compound cures chemically without special equipment. These simple molds are not quite as durable as vulcanized rubber and can lose detail because of bubbles.

Mold frames can be bought or made, using a strip of aluminum and glass or plastic sheet. When the model is in position, hold the sheets in place with rubber bands or a C-clamp. Mix the compound thoroughly according to the manufactuer's directions. Allow the mold to cure then cut it open to remove the model.

Problem Solving

Problem   The casting is covered with warts.

Reason   There were air bubbles in the investment. Unfortunately, these voids often lodge in details, where they are difficult to cut away.

Solution   Make the investment thicker next time, and extend the vacuum time. For now, cut away the beads with snips, a graver or grind with a flex shaft bur.

Problem   Incomplete casting. Ouch!

Reason   If there is a large button, this means that the metal wasn't fully melted and didn't get into the mold. If only the top portion of the casting fills, this might mean there simply wasn't enough metal. If the edges of the partial casting are round, it probably means the metal encountered air trapped in the mold cavity.

Solution   Learn from the mistake by thinking through exactly what happened until you understand the logic of the problem.

Problem   Porosity.

Reason   As the metal cools it pulls itself into a more compact structure, creating microscopic spaces. Because there was no additional metal coming into this region, the spaces were not filled.

Solution   Sprue to the thickest part of the piece and make the sprue thicker than the area to which it attaches.

Problem   When I quench the mold, not much happens. It's taking me a long time to scrape the hard investment off the casting.

Reason   You are waiting too long between completing the casting and quenching. Usually about a minute is enough.

Solution   This is not a problem, except for the increased chore of removing investment. Heat the casting with a torch and quench it in water, but be careful not to breathe the silica-laden vapors.

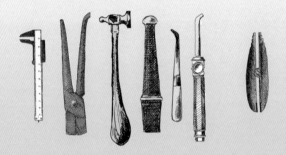

Chapter 7

Stones & Stonesetting

General Information

Introduction

Lapidary, the art of working with gemstones, is a complex field of study all by itself, and few metalsmiths can give it as much time as they would like. The following pages make an attempt to provide some working knowledge for those who deal with stones as a complementary aspect of their craft. It is not complete, but will lay a foundation for further investigation. This chapter contains an alphabetical list of fifty popular stones with some information, history, or tips for each one, and in some cases, the magical qualities ascribed to specific stones. No guarantees are offered, but who knows.

Birthstones

Today the commercial jewelry industry has effectively blunted any charm or seriousness concerning the relationship between earth materials and the season of one's birth. There was a time, however, when such relationships played an important part in daily life. The list below is borrowed from *The Curious Lore of Precious Stones* by George Frederick Kunz (Dover 1971), a book that is recommended for further investigation.

Birthstones

January	Garnet, sapphire
February	Amethyst, sapphire
March	Bloodstone, jasper
April	Diamond, sapphire
May	Agate, emerald, chalcedony, carnelian
June	Emerald, agate, pearl, chalcedony, turquoise
July	Ruby, carnelian, onyx, sardonyx, turquoise
August	Carnelian, moonstone, topaz, alexandrite
September	Sapphire, lapis lazuli, coral
October	Opal, aquamarine, beryl
November	Topaz, pearl
December	Turquoise, ruby, bloodstone

Wedding Anniversary Tokens

Year	Token
1	rose, beryl, paper
2	crystal, cotton
3	chrysoprase, leather
4	moonstone, silk
5	carnelian, wood
6	peridot, sugar
7	coral, wool
8	opal, clay
9	citrine, willow
10	turquoise, tin
11	garnet
12	amethyst, linen
13	agate
14	ivory, lace
15	topaz
25	silver
30	pearl
35	jade
40	ruby
45	sapphire
50	golden
55	emerald
60	diamond

Cuts & Hardness

Gem Evaluation

> Color   In many cases, such as agates, color is entirely a matter of taste. In others, such as emerald, a deep color is a major factor in value.

> Cut   The planes or curves should be symmetrical, well polished, and arranged to complement the material.

> Hardness   A gem that will not retain its polish is of limited value to jewelers. In setting, it is important to know the hardness of the material being used. Soft stones should be set in a way that will protect them.

> Light   Cat's-eye and iridescence are examples of this.

> Luster   Brightness of the shine—some stones have a lesser value because they will not polish.

> Inclusions   Some stones, such as rutilated quartz or moss agate, are valued for their inclusions. In other stones, such as amethyst, inclusions lower the value.

---

standard cabochon (cab)

high cab (bullet)

double cab (lentil)

buff top

rose cut

marquise

baguette

tapered baguette

Mohs Scale of Hardness

Each material will scratch those with a lower number and will be scratched by those with a higher number. The steps along the scale are not regular. For example, #2 and #3 are close in hardness while #10, diamond, is 80 times harder than #9.

1	talc
2	gypsum
3	calcite
4	fluorite
5	apatite
6	orthoclase
7	quartz
8	topaz
9	corundum
10	diamond

Summary

Name	Hardness	O/T *	Heat Sensitive	Notes
agate	7	O	yes	often banded
alexandrite	8–9	T		changes color
amber	2	both	very	organic
amethyst	7	T	yes	
ametrine	7	T		bicolor
ammonite	7	O	yes	fossilized shells
aquamarine	8	T	very	
aventurine	7	O	yes	sparkles
carnelian	7	O	yes	
chalcedony	7	O	yes	
chrome diopside	5½–6	T		
chrysoberyl	8	both		
chrysocolla	6	O	yes	
chrysoprase	6	O	yes	
citrine	7	T	yes	
coral	3	O	very	organic
corundum	9	T		
cubic zirconia	9	T		recent synthetic
diamond	10	T		
emerald	8	both	yes	cleaves easily
garnet	7	T	yes	
hematite	6	O		
iolite	7–7½	T		pleochroic
ivory	2	O	very	organic
jade	6	O	yes	greasy luster
jasper	7	O		
jet	4	O	very	organic
labradorite	6	O	very	iridescent
lapis lazuli	6	O	yes	
malachite	3½–4	O	very	often banded
moissanite	9½	T	no	second hardest
moonstone	6	T	yes	adularescent
onyx	7	O	yes	
opal	6	T	very	interior colors
pearl	3	O	very	
peridot	7	T	yes	
quartz	7	both		
rhodochrosite	4	T	yes	
ruby	9	both		star or cat's-eye
sapphire	9	both		star or cat's-eye
sardonyx	7	O	yes	
serpentine	2–6	O		dust has asbestos
sodalite	6	O		
spinel	8	T		
tanzanite	6½–7	T		pleochroic
tiger's-eye	7	O	yes	silky interior
topaz	8	T	yes	cleaves easily
tourmaline	7	T	yes	dichroic
turquoise	6	O	yes	
zircon	7	T		cleaves easily

Opaque or Transparent

Gemstones

AGATE (Ag it)
Hardness: 7

> A type of chalcedony; a cryptocrystalline quartz. This means the crystals are so tiny they do not show up under normal magnification.

Green	Relief from eye trouble.
Green with stripes	A woman who drinks water in which such a ring has been washed will never be sterile.
Moss agate	Also called dendritic (Greek, *dendron*, "tree"); worn by a farmer on the upper arm to ensure a good harvest; placed on right horn of oxen to protect them.

ALEXANDRITE (al x ZAN drite)
Hardness: 8½

> This natural stone is a type of chrysoberyl that shows a range of transparent colors, from blue in daylight to reddish-yellow in artificial light.

> A synthetic stone, more widely available, is actually a treated corundum, H9.
> The stone was named for Czar Alexander II who, according to legend, came of legal age on the day the stone was discovered.

AMBER (AM bur)
Hardness: 2–2½

> This is not a stone but the naturally hardened resin of the amber pine, *Pinus succinifera*. Transparent amber is 120–180 million years old. Opaque amber, called copal, is 60 million years old.
> The name comes from the Arabic *anbar*. The Greeks called it *elektrum* from the Phoenician word for sun/golden. Because amber will hold a charge, this gave us our word *electric*. Rub it on a sweater and it will hold enough static electricity to lift hair or bits of paper.

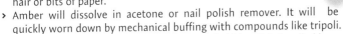

> Amber will dissolve in acetone or nail polish remover. It will be quickly worn down by mechanical buffing with compounds like tripoli.
> Some amber contains thousands of tiny air bubbles. This is called bone amber and can be cleared by heating in mineral oil.
> Amber is easy to fake. To test a sample:
>   • Brush it with methyl alcohol or ethyl acetate. Nonfossil resins (a.k.a. plastics) will dissolve.
>   • Set a sample into brine: real amber will float but artificial amber will sink.
>   • Touch a sample with a hot needle. The smoke created will smell either like a pine woods or a plastics factory.

Gemstones

AMETHYST (AM e thist)
Hardness: 7

> Amethyst is a form of quartz. The top grade is a deep purple and has no flaws or inclusions.
> When heated to around 1000° F (540° C) amethysts turn dark yellow or reddish-brown and are called citrines. Because they are more richly colored than natural citrines, they are more expensive.

AMETRINE (AM e treen)
Hardness: 7

> Unique bicolor quartz crystals of amethyst and citrine that grow together.
> These stones come from the Anahí Mine in Bolivia.
> Citrine is associated with the third chakra (self-esteem) while amethyst is connected to intuition and introspection. The stone signifies the transition between corporeal and spiritual attributes.

AMMONITE (AM o nyt)
Hardness: 7

> Ammonite is a cephalopod (phylum *Mollusca*) that once swam in shallow marine seas, and became extinct at the end of the Cretaceous period about 65 million years ago (along with the dinosaurs). The closest living relative to the ammonite is the chambered nautilus.

AQUAMARINE (AUKWA mareen)
Hardness: 7½–8

> The name comes from the Latin *beryllus aquamarinus,* "beryl resembling seawater."
> This gem increased in popularity around 1920 when heat treatment was developed to turn pale blue-green stones into deeper blue shades.

AVENTURINE (a VENT chu reen)
Hardness: 7

> A fine-grained quartz with many flake inclusions, occurring in several colors, mainly green, brown, and gray.
> The characteristic sparkle of this stone is called aventurescence.

CARNELIAN (kar NEEL yan)
Hardness: 6½–7

> The color of this red chalcedony is due to the presence of iron.
> The opaque variety is called sard. When it occurs in brown and white layers it is called sardonyx.
> Carnelian was said to stop nosebleeds and to prevent blood rising to the head.

Gemstones

CHALCEDONY (kal SED nee) Hardness: 6½–7

> A cryptocrystalline quartz—that is, quartz with very tiny crystals. Carnelian, onyx, agates, and chrysoprase are all forms of chalcedony.
> In the world of jewelry, the word refers to a light-blue, translucent stone. These stones may be made by dyeing agates but the naturally occurring variety is more desirable.

CHROME DIOPSIDE (krom dy OP syd) Hardness: 5½–6

> These translucent gems have a vivid green color.
> The primary source is Siberia, Russia.
> Though mined for decades, it is only recently that the gem is receiving widespread attention.

CHRYSOBERYL (KRIS o burl) Hardness: 8½

> This stone occurs in both a transparent and a cloudy variety, and can be yellow, green or brown. Clear stones are usually faceted, while the cloudy specimens are cut as cabochons.

CHRYSOCOLLA (kris o KOL La) Hardness: 5–6

> From the Greek *chrysos* (gold) and *kolla* (glue). In ancient usage the term included malachite. Both were used as a flux for soldering and fusing gold.
> Chrysocolla from the site of King Solomon's Mines in Eilat, Israel, is called Eilat (Elat) stone.
> Because this is a copper-bearing ore it will be damaged by pickles that are designed to attack copper oxides (e.g., Sparex).

CHRYSOPRASE (KRIS o prayz) Hardness: 6½–7

> A light-green, translucent chalcedony; the most valuable of the chalcedony family.
> From the Greek words for "gold" and "leek," referring to its golden-green color, which is caused by nickel salts.

CITRINE (SI treen) Hardness: 7

> This yellow quartz can be found naturally or made by heating amethyst (purple quartz) to around 1000° F (140° C).
> The yellow-brown form is called "cairngorm" after the place of origin in Scotland.
> Dark reddish-brown quartz is called *sang de boeuf*, French for "ox blood."

Gemstones

CORAL (KOR l)
Hardness: 3½

> This is not a stone in the usual sense but a rock-like material formed from the underwater deposit of many tiny skeletons of invertebrate animals.
> This is a soft material and should be treated gently. It will not tolerate harsh cleansers, abrasion or heat.

CORUNDUM (kor UN dum)
Hardness: 9

> Until the Middle Ages corundum was called "hyacinth" and was thought to exist only as a blue stone. When it was discovered that other colors of corundum existed, the name sapphire was used for the blue variety.

CUBIC ZIRCONIUM (KU bik zir KON iyum)
Hardness: 8½

> A transparent, singly refractive, man-made gem produced from the element zirconium.
> It is available in many colors, as well as a bright white that resembles diamond. Because of its fire and low cost, CZ has replaced other contenders as a diamond substitute.

DIAMOND (DI mund)
Hardness: 10

> From the Greek *adamas*, "unbreakable, indomitable."
> Diamond powder was at one time considered to be medicinal. In 1532, physicians administered gem powders, including diamond, to the ailing Pope Clement VII. Didn't work.
> Diamond has long been credited with powers in keeping with its unique properties. It is said that diamonds will drive away madness, night spirits and evil dreams. Diamonds will promote virtue, generosity, and courage, and are said to protect a house from lightning and other natural disasters.
> In ancient times, diamonds were found only in India and were not highly regarded because they could only be used in their natural octahedral shape. In 1456, Louis de Berqueur developed a way to cut facets that revealed the brilliance of the gem, and led to increased popularity. By the European Renaissance, noblemen and ladies were wearing the highly fashionable gem. In subsequent waves of discovery, diamonds were mined in Brazil (1720s), and South Africa (1860s).

Gemstones

EMERALD (EM e ruld) Hardness: 7½–8

> A bright green beryl, very valuable if free of inclusions and of strong color.
> Inclusions are called the *jardin* (garden) of the stone.
> Emeralds are notoriously brittle and require great care in setting. For this reason faceted stones with a thick girdle are preferred.
> Do not clean emeralds in an ultrasonic machine. The solution may penetrate the stone and cause it to shatter.
> Linked to fertility and the Earth goddess, emerald is a birthstone of spring (May). Sacred to the goddess Venus, it is worn by women to ease childbirth.
> The sight of an emerald is said to bring such terror to a viper or cobra that their eyes leap out of their heads.

GARNET (GAR net) Hardness: 6½–7½

> From the Latin *granum*, "grain or pip," which in turn, came from the Phoenician word for pomegranate, *punica granatum*.
> When worn on the body, garnets are said to prevent skin diseases.
> Garnet assures the wearer of love, faithfulness and safety from wounds.
> When danger approaches, the stone loses its brilliance.
> Garnets will protect the wearer from evil and from terrifying dreams.
> For obvious reasons, red garnets have been associated with blood. As recently as 1892, native soldiers in Kashmir fought the British with bullets made of garnet in the belief that these would magically find their way to their targets.

Types of garnets:

— *Pyrope* – a deep red color. Its name in Greek means "fiery eye."
— *Almadine* – dark red with a tinge of mauve. The especially purple variety is called rhodolite.
— *Spessartite* – red-orange or orange-brown; shows internal wavy veil of fluid contained in the stone; rare and expensive.
— *Grossular (Grossularite)* – a speckled green stone resembling jade. Hessonite is a subspecies.
— *Uvarovite* – Rare, intensely green stone.
— *Andradite* – This species of garnet contains iron; it is rarely cut.

Gemstones

HEMATITE (HE ma tite)
Hardness: 5½–6½

> A lustrous black stone often cut with facets or carved with a warrior's head.
> Though the stone is black, it will leave a red streak when scratched along a rough surface. The stone appears to bleed, and so takes its name from the Greek word for blood, *haima*.
> Hematite (also spelled "haematite") is the world's most important iron ore.

IOLITE (I o lyt)
Hardness: 7–7½

> These gems show a deep blue with a hint of purple.
> Iolite is strongly dichroic, which means it shows different colors depending on the angle of viewing.

IVORY (I vree)
Hardness: 2½

> Ivory comes from the tusks of elephants and is becoming increasingly rare as the elephant approaches extinction. In many parts of the world it is illegal to use ivory.
> Other similar materials should be identified with an adjective, such as whale ivory, or better, faux ivory.

JADE (JAYD)
Hardness: 7

> The word refers to two distinct minerals not differentiated until 1863. These are properly called *jadeite* and *nephrite*.
> Jade occurs in white (muttonfat jade), yellow, lavender, earthy brown, and black, as well as the familiar greens.
> Spanish conquistadors found many objects of carved jade and, believing it to ease kidney pains, called it *piedra de ijada* (loin stone). European doctors called it *palis nephriticus* from the Greek *nephros*, kidney.

JASPER (JAS pur)
Hardness: 6½–7

> From the Hebrew *yashpeh* and Assyrian *yashpu*; referred to in cuneiform writings of 1500 BC. Originally the word referred to any green stone.
> Jasper occurs in many colors and patterns, including stripes and pictures. These are really fossilized algae made when decomposed organic matter was replaced by silicon oxide.

Gemstones

JET (JET)
Hardness: 3–4

> A dense black coal found in many places around the world; especially popular during the reign of Queen Victoria, who wore jewelry of carved jet in her 40-year mourning for her deceased husband. Most British jet came from the town of Whitby.
> Burnt and powdered jet is said to drive away snakes and reptiles, and to heal toothaches and headaches.

LABRADORITE (LAB bra dor ite)
Hardness: 6

> This is a blue iridescent feldspar found in Labrador.
> A similar gem mined in Finland shows a wider range of colors and is called *spectrolite*.
> Black moonstone is usually labradorite from Madagascar.

LAPIS LAZULI (LAP is LAZ u lee)
Hardness: 5–6

> From the Latin *lapis*, "stone" and Arabic *lazuli*, "blue".
> Known for its deep blue color, sometimes found with flecks of gold-colored pyrite or whitish-gray mottlings of calcite.
> Lapis is still being mined at the oldest mines in the world, located in Iraq. When mining began there 6000 years ago, the country was called Babylon. Think of that.
> Lapis was sent to Egypt as tribute. There it was carved to make cylinder seals and ground to a powder for eye makeup.
> In ancient Egypt, the stone was symbolic of truth (Ma) and was worn by the chief justice.
> From the Middle Ages through the 19th century, painters mixed oil with powdered lapis to make the color we call ultramarine.
> The gem is believed to ease eye troubles, treat asthma, induce sleep and relieve anxiety.

MALACHITE (MAL a kite)
Hardness: 5–6

> A copper ore made up of deep and pale green stripes or concentric circles.
> Malachite powder was used in ancient times as eye makeup.
> It was commonly held to ease labor, protect infants and children, and soothe their pain when they were cutting teeth.
> Because of its high copper content, malachite will be damaged by jewelers pickle.

Gemstones

MOISSANITE (MOY zan yt)
Hardness: 9½

> This man-made gem traces its origins to the discovery of silicon carbide in 1893 by Henri Moissan. The fragments he found in a meteor in Arizona, which were too small for practical use, proved that such a compound was possible.
> It is second in hardness only to diamond.
> Created in a near-colorless version and a pale green version.
> Moissanite is roughly 20–30% the cost of diamonds.

MOONSTONE (MOON ston)
Hardness: 6–6½

> A feldspar of orthoclase with thin layers of albite. This yields a play of light called adularescence, as light is spread by the fine particles or layers.
> Moonstone occurs in white, gray, pink, green, blue, chocolate, and an almost clear variety that looks like a water droplet.
> When worn around the neck, moonstone is believed to protect against epilepsy and sunstroke. It is used to treat headaches and nosebleeds.

ONYX (ON ix)
Hardness: 6½–7

> A chalcedony composed of black and white bands. In common usage the term often refers to an agate dyed uniformly black.
> Onyx with brown and white bands is called sardonyx.
> When cut to show concentric circles, onyx forms an eye-like amulet that was worn by the Sumerians, Greeks, Egyptians and Romans to ward off evil.
> The Arabic name for this stone, *el jaza*, means sadness.

OPAL (O pl)
Hardness: 5½–6½

> From the Sanskrit *upala*, gem.
> A highly praised stone that shows a range of color flashes, usually including red, blue, green and violet.
> Opal is hydrated silicon dioxide. The play of colors is the result of water (1–15% by weight) trapped in the stone. Care should be taken that opals do not dry out. A periodic coating of baby oil is recommended.
> Opals from Mexico and Brazil usually contain more water and are less stable than Australian opals.

Gemstones

Types of Opal:
> - Fire – bright orange-red; translucent to transparent.
> - Flame – as above when showing red.
> - Flash – undivided flashes of a single color.
> - Harlequin – a mosaic of iridescent color.
> - Pinpoint – a multitude of tiny specks of many colors.
> - Matrix – stone cut so as to leave the opal attached to the rock in which it was formed.
> - Doublet – opal glued to a backing of obsidian or onyx.
> - Triplet – a doublet with rock crystal glued on top to increase luster and strength.

PEARL (PURL)   Hardness: 2½–4

> - A lustrous deposit formed inside a living bivalve mollusk, often in response to an irritation felt by the animal. Though many mollusks form such deposits, most species do not make pearls with attractive surfaces.
> - Pearls are formed in saltwater and freshwater bivalve mollusks. They are identified by their place of origin, for instance, Mississippi River.
> - The largest source of pearls is Lake Biwa in Japan, where extensive pearl farming is done.
> - Pearls sometimes grow attached to the shell of the animal, rather than in its tissue. These are called blister pearls.
> - Cultured or cultivated pearls are made inside a mollusk but have human help to get started. A bit of tissue or a bead is inserted in the animal and allowed to collect nacreous secretions for about four years.
> - Pearls are attributed to Venus as the symbol of innocence.
> - Tie knots between pearls when stringing to keep them from rubbing against one another.

PERIDOT (PER i doh)   Hardness: 7

> - A transparent gem, sometimes called chrysolite, occurring as pale to deep yellow-green.
> - Peridot is associated with the astrological sign of Libra (September 22–October 23) and is assigned to the sun.
> - In ancient Hebrew writings this stone is linked with the Tribe of Simeon.
> - Peridot is believed to cure liver disease and dropsy, to free the mind from envious thoughts, and to dispel terrors of the night. For full magical power it should be set in gold.

Gemstones

QUARTZ (KORTZ)   Hardness: 7
> Quartz is the most common of all minerals and accounts
> for as much as 12% of the volume of the earth's crust.
> There are two forms:
>> a) crystalline, a single crystal that is generally transparent
>> and either clear (rock crystal) or colored by minerals to be purple
>> (amethyst), yellow (citrine), or brown (smoky quartz).
>> b) chalcedony, a microcrystalline version that is usually translucent.
>> Examples include flint, onyx, aventurine, jasper, carnelian, agate,
>> and chrysoprase.

RHODOCHROSITE (rodo KRO zite)   Hardness: 3½–4½
> A bright luminous pink gem often banded with white stripes.
> Rhodochrosite is an ore of manganese; its chemical
> formula is $MnCO_3$.
> Found in many sites around the world with the best
> specimens coming from Colorado.

RUBY (ROO bee)   Hardness: 9
> A corundum that occurs as a transparent deep red stone
> and as an opaque reddish-gray material. In this form it may
> exhibit a star (asterism) or a single-line chatoyancy.
> When flawless, a ruby is more valuable than a diamond
> of equal weight.
> Synthetic rubies are used for jewelry, bearings and laser equipment.

SAPPHIRE (SAF ire)   Hardness: 9
> This form of corundum can occur as blue, yellow, pink,
> brown, black, lilac, and green, both as transparent and
> opaque, the latter sometimes showing a star (asterism) or
> cat's-eye (chatoyancy).
> Until the Middle Ages, sapphires were called hyacinths because of
> their pale blue color. When it was realized that the mineral occurred
> in other colors, the term sapphire was adopted for the blue variety
> while others use a color description, e.g., yellow sapphire.

SARDONYX (sar DON ix)   Hardness: 6½–7
> A kind of chalcedony made brown by the presence of iron.
> Sardonyx was a popular stone in ancient times and was
> credited with many powers, such as the ability to protect
> against snake bites, witchcraft and sorcery.

Gemstones

SERPENTINE (SURP en teen)   Hardness: 2–6

> An opaque green stone with mottled reddish-brown or milky patches. This, along with its waxy appearance, makes it look like snakeskin (hence the name).

> Drinking medicine from a serpentine vessel was thought to increase the healing power of the medicine.

SODALITE (SO da lite)   Hardness: 6–7

> A popular opaque stone most widely known for its blue color, which somewhat resembles lapis lazuli.

> White and grayish-white mottlings are often found in sodalite; in poor grade material these will be obvious.

SPINEL (spin ELL)   Hardness: 8

> A transparent stone of red (the most valuable), pink, green, blue-green and purple.

> Synthetic spinel is produced in large quantities and is associated with inexpensive jewelry in imitation of diamonds, aquamarine, sapphires, and other gems. Air bubbles inside the stone often betray these synthetics.

TANZANITE (TANZ neyt)   Hardness: 6–7

> This light violet to blue-colored gem is trichroic, which means it can show three distinct colors depending on the angle of viewing.

> This stone, discovered in Tanzania in 1967, is particularly sensitive to ultrasound and should never be cleaned in an ultrasonic cleaner.

> Tanzanite is similar to iolite, which is also pleochroic.

> Most samples are heat treated to achieve a dark blue.

TIGER'S-EYE (TY gerz I)   Hardness: 6½–7

> Blue, violet, and golden brown translucent stones showing a silky interior that shimmers as the stone is rotated. It can sometimes be cut to show a cat's-eye.

> The effect is the result of asbestos fibers that have been partially replaced by quartz.

> When the fibers are coarse, the stone is called a hawk's eye.

Gemstones

TOPAZ (TOW paz)

Hardness: 8

> A transparent stone usually of golden yellow but also occurring as pink, red, blue, green and colorless specimens.
> In ancient times the word topaz referred to several other stones; today it is often mistakenly used for smoky quartz and citrine.
> Rubbing or gentle heating of topaz electrifies it, causing it to attract bits of paper or hair.

TOURMALINE (TUR ma leen)

Hardness: 7–7½

> A transparent stone of many colors, most notably green, blue-green and pink.
> Often several colors appear side by side. Crystals cut to reveal a pink semicircle with a green rim are called watermelon tourmaline.
> Tourmaline is dichromatic; it shows a bright color from one direction but will look almost black when seen from another. Like topaz, this stone will hold static electricity when rubbed.

TURQUOISE (TUR kwoyz)

Hardness: 5–6

> A blue or blue-green stone, usually opaque.
> From French *pierre turquoise* which means Turkish stone, a reference to its popular use in Turkey. Arabs call it *fayruz* or *firusaj*, the lucky stone.
> Blue material will turn green as it absorbs oil from the skin. After polishing, most turquoise is sealed with a plastic that soaks into the stone and closes the pores. This is called stabilizing.
> Some pieces of turquoise are cut so as to contain some of the rock in which they were formed. This is called matrix turquoise. Some varieties show fine dark lines running throughout the stone; this is called spiderweb turquoise.

ZIRCON (ZIR kon)

Hardness: 7–7½

> A transparent brittle stone occurring as brownish or green material, usually heated to turn it pale yellow and blue. It can be found naturally colored as orange-red (most valuable), purple, reddish-brown, and brownish-yellow.
> Zircon is said to drive away evil spirits and bad dreams, to banish grief and melancholy, restore appetite, induce sleep and protect against lightning.

Basic Bezel

Basic Box Bezel

A bezel is a thin band of metal that surrounds a stone and is pressed over its edge to hold it in place. It is probably the oldest and most widely used setting in the world.

. Wrap bezel wire or a similar strip of metal around the stone; mark, and cut. For small stones, bend the loop by eye and fit to the stone. For larger stones. bend the metal directly on the stone.

2. File the ends to make a tight fit. Use as little solder as possible— solder alloys are stiff and difficult to push over a stone.

3. Check the fit. If the bezel is too small, stretch it on a tapered mandrel or by planishing with a steel hammer. If it is too loose, remove a piece of bezel and resolder.

4. File or sand to the correct height.

5. File or sand a knife edge around the top of the bezel. Stop just before the rim disappears. If this is lost, it's easy to go too far.

6. Rub the bezel on sandpaper to true and clean the bottom edge, then recheck the fit. After soldering to a flat sheet, pickle and check the joint. It is important that the bezel is attached all the way around.

7. Where applicable, trim away excess sheet, using a saw or scissors. To avoid bending with the scissors, cut on tangents.

8. Solder the bezel into position on the workpiece.

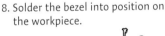

Tube Setting & Thick Bezels

Tube Setting

If the tubing has a thick wall, cut a bearing with a setting bur or a thin graver. In a pinch you can use a standard drill bit of the proper size.

If the tube wall is too thin for this, draw down a piece of the tube so it slides into the first piece to make a bearing.

To set stones in a production situation, buy or make a rod with a hemispherical depression on its end. Mount this in a flex shaft, lubricate with light oil, and press it over the tube while rotating at a slow to medium speed.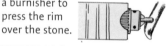

You can set the diamonds into tubes, then solder the setting into position. Mount the tube in a flex shaft, and hold a bur against it. Press the diamond into the seat and rotate the tube against a burnisher to press the rim over the stone.

Thick Bezels

Construct a bezel as you would for a box bezel, but use a thicker wall, for instance, 18 gauge for a stone under 5 mm and 16 gauge for a larger one. Push the bezel wall over the stone with a planishing punch. Use a chasing hammer with repeated light taps.

- The object must be firmly anchored. Use a pitch pot, engraver's ball, shellac, or sealing wax on a board, or grip the work in a vise. Support rings on a wooden wedge or in a ring clamp.
- Lock the stone in place with four sharp blows evenly spaced around the bezel. In successive courses around the stone, raise the angle of the tool until it is vertical.
- Use a planishing punch around the bezel to smooth away hammer marks. Define the shape with a file or a pumice wheel—no sandpaper! Buff the collar either by machine or with a polishing stick. The profile can be rounded or have crisp angles.

Tooled Edge

Start with a bezel made of thick metal. Grip the work securely as described above and push the bezel over the stone. When the bezel is pressed uniformly onto the stone, hold the tool vertically and move it around the bezel with many light taps, creating the pattern.

Fancy Bezels

Step Bezel

This backless bezel has several advantages: it uses less material, saving cost and reducing weight. It can be faster to make than a box bezel, and it reveals the back of the gem. Here are four approaches:

Step bezel is available commercially in fine silver and 14K gold, plain or as a fancy style called gallery step bezel.

You can also create the step bezel by soldering two strips together before bending the bezel around the stone. A variation on this is to use half-round or square wires to provide the ledge.

Make a bezel that fits the stone, then make a second ring (bearing) that fits snugly inside the first. For faceted stones, file a bevel on the inner ring before soldering the two pieces together.

Make the bezel of heavy stock such as 16 or 18 gauge, then cut a bearing with flex shaft tools or gravers.

Raised Bezels

Make a bezel that has most of the back open. You can do this by soldering the bezel to a sheet and then cutting out the interior space, or by soldering a ring of square or rectangular wire inside the bezel.

Make a small conical section whose larger diameter is the same as that of the bezel, either by bending an arc or by soldering a loop closed and forming it in a dapping block.

Solder short lengths of wire or tubing onto the underside of the bezel at regular intervals.

Rub the spacers on sandpaper to make sure each one has a flat face. Solder the cone onto the spacers, then cut and file them flush with the bezel. For a ring, cut the cone to accommodate the curve of a finger.

Prong Settings

Basket Settings

1. Bend two V-shapes of wire and prop them up on the soldering block. Solder the points where they contact each other. To make a six-prong head, use three V-shapes.

2. Make a ring to hold the prongs together. This can go on the inside (subtle) or outside (decorative). The inside ring is smaller than the stone's diameter; the outside ring is made to fit around the stone.

3. Attach the head to the workpiece, then pickle and polish. Cut a bearing, trim the prongs to the correct height and set the stone as usual.

Turtle Settings

This basic and versatile setting offers huge possibilities. In its simplest form, it is nothing more than a tracing of the stone with four tabs (legs) added to become prongs. This shape is sawn out of sheet metal (add a head for a pendant loop) and bent to clutch the stone.

The first two examples are sawn from sheet, the second is made of wire, while the third example uses both. The green areas indicate the size of the stone they are built to hold. Often the tips of the prongs are planished or filed to make them more graceful.

Variations

- For irregular stones, emphasize the asymmetry with prongs of different sizes and uneven spacing.
- Ornament the prongs with piercing, filework or overlay.
- Decorate the back plate by piercing, roll printing, stamping or overlay.
- On thick metal, score the bend, bring the prong perpendicular, then reinforce the scored area with solder.
- Use a single piece to set two stones back to back.
- Cut the base larger than the stone to create a rim around the gem.

Pedestal-Prong

Pedestal-Prong

This setting can be made with 3, 4, 5, or 6 prongs and can be used with cabs or faceted stones. It is one of the few settings that looks good with asymmetrical or different-sized prongs.

1. Make a ring of 16–20 B&S sheet. The outside diameter should equal the diameter of the stone.

2. For a faceted stone, file a bevel around the inside edge of this ring. For round stones, you can use a setting bur; for others, use a cylinder bur or a needle file.

3. Cut oversize lengths of square or half-round wire for prongs. File a point on each one.

4. Push the prong wires into a charcoal block or soldering pad around the pedestal and solder them into position.

5. Pickle, rinse and check the prongs for symmetry and strength, then trim off the extra material. File the bottom edge and adjust the prong height to make the setting uniform.

6. Attach to the body of the piece, shape the prongs, and set the stone with either a pusher or pliers.

Variations

One of the best things about this setting is its versatility. Use it for symmetrical and irregular stones, for delicate and large prongs, and for any size gem.

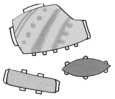

Back to Back

In the construction method described above, a natural by-product is a setting with prongs on both sides. Use this to set matching stones back to back, or cut the setting in half to make two matching parts.

Crowns & Collets

Crown Setting

The basic unit of this setting is a cone. These can be fabricated by bending sheet, or made in a bezel block—a steel tool that consists of a heavy plate with a series of conical holes, and corresponding tapered punches.

1. Fabricate a cone that will enclose the stone.
2. After truing the cone on a mandrel, mark out prongs, first from a top view and then on the sides. Locate the prongs so most of the soldered joint will be cut away. Use dividers to mark a line parallel to the base.
3. With a saw, cut away the area between the prongs. To hold for sawing, mount the cone on a dowel with sealing wax or shellac, or hold it in pliers that have been specially shaped for this. Use a round file or a bud-bur to make the prongs neat and even.
4. Invert the head and repeat the last step, this time cutting away the area between the prongs. This is not necessary for small stones.
5. If you've cut out areas from the bottom, make a ring to become the base of the setting. Use square wire or flatten a ring made from round wire so it will make positive contact with the base of the crown. In large settings, saw off the lower section of the cone, and put it carefully aside. After cutting decorative sections below the prongs, solder the lower section back into place.

Collet

1. Lay out an arc as described in the Appendix. For small stones, accuracy by eye is often sufficient.
2. Bend the arc into a cone and close it with hard solder.
3. True up the cone on a small mandrel (often a scribe or centerpunch). Set the cone across open vise jaws to stretch it.
4. File a flat surface on the outside of the cone for each prong. Keep the spacing even.
5. Cut tapered prongs from 18–22 gauge sheet.
6. Solder the prongs in place on the collet. Poke the prong strips into the soldering block to hold them into position.
7. Pickle, rinse, and check the fit. The stone should not rest on the collet. If it does, the collet is too big or the angle of the cone is too steep.
8. Solder the collet to the piece, polish, and cut bearings in each prong.

Frames

Making a Square or Rectangular Frame

Many settings require a frame that is a perfect fit for the stone. Lack of precision at this early stage will almost always make subsequent steps difficult or impossible. The following method is a standard approach, whether making a tiny setting or a large container.

1. Cut off a piece of flattened wire or strip, a little longer than two adjacent sides. File a notch with a square file and bend the strip into an L shape. After checking with a square to be sure the corner is exactly 90°, solder the corner. Make two of these shapes.

2. Measure and cut the small side so its length will equal the desired interior dimension of the box. Repeat this with the other unit, then hold them side by side to be certain they are equal.

3. Slide the two L-shaped pieces together and mark the place at which they make a frame that is exactly the desired length. Place the solder outside the joint

4. After soldering, cut away the excess metal and file the sides smooth.

A Versatile Base

1. Follow the directions above to make two identical frames.

2. File away the corners of one of them, handling the piece gently as it becomes more fragile.

3. When each corner shows a V, use a small file or a piece of folded sandpaper to bevel the interior faces of each corner. Tilt each side inward until the corners touch. Solder these joints.

4. Rub the resulting pyramid shape to clean and refine its larger edge, then solder it onto the other box.

There are several uses for this box:

Attach wire to use the box as bezel.

Solder prongs in corners for a rectangular stone.

File off corners, one at a time, and replace with sheet.

Stringing

String

Whatever string you use, be certain that it fills the bead hole or the resulting strand will be sloppy and insecure. Ordinary sewing thread can be used, but it is generally too thin for most beads. Likewise, dental floss can be used, but because it is flattened, it isn't the best choice. Beading cord is produced in nylon threads in about a dozen sizes and many colors. These are often sold on small cards in short lengths that have a needle permanently affixed to one end. The traditional choice (and still probably the best) is silk cord. It resists stretching and is sold in many bright colors and a wide range of sizes. The thinnest cord is called #00; sizes move up the alphabet through A, B, and C as they get bigger. From F the series goes to FF and then FFF, which is the thickest silk available.

Stringing Equipment

> Use tweezers to hold beads as you work. Protect against scratching soft stones and glass with a couple of layers of nail polish.
> A needle tool is handy for guiding the location of knots and poking old bits of string out of bead holes. A biology needle works well, or a sewing needle can be taped to a pencil. Soften the point by sanding it.
> To hold the beads, use a piece of flannel taped to a board or a piece of stiff paper folded into ridges. If you're doing a lot of stringing, buy a plastic bead tray.

Bead Tips

After stringing, the cord is generally tied off and attached to a hook of some sort. These findings can be bought ready-made or fabricated at the bench. A typical ending is a small device called a bead tip that consists of a small cup with an attached finger. The knot of the cord is settled into the cup and the tip is bent over to hide it as it clutches the finding. An alternate method uses a simple piece of tubing to crimp onto the cord. This can be done with round-nose pliers or dull snips. In either case, lay a dab of glue or nail polish on the knot.

Chapter 8
Mechanisms

Earring Findings

General Information
- Some people can wear only gold or stainless wires, but most people can wear sterling earwires and posts.
- 22 gauge wire is usually a comfortable thickness.
- Work-harden wires by twisting them.
- Standard length of posts is 9 mm (⅜").

Making Friction Backs
1. Cut a strip of 24–gauge sterling (26–gauge gold) about 12 mm long.
2. Strike a sharp punch in the center to form a funnel-like depression. Drill a hole in the center, equal to the diameter of the ear post.
3. Make a grip by filing notches. Polish.
5. Bend the wings up with round-nose pliers, making sure they curl at least three-quarters of a circle. Adjust the gap between the wings to create tension on the post.
6. Make a groove about 1–2 millimeters from the end of the post by pinching with round-nose pliers. This groove will stop the nut from sliding off the end of the post.

Omega Clips
These elegant earring findings have become the standard for upscale earrings.

They replace a friction nut with a spring-tension loop that folds down against the back of the lobe to hold the earring in place. Omega clips can be bought ready to attach or made from scratch. Do not snap the loop into place until all soldering is complete so the wire remains springy.

And what would we call this letter of the Greek alphabet?

Clips for Nonpierced Ears
Like Omega clips, these can be purchased or made in the studio. In this design the center finger presses down on the vertical wall to create the tension that snaps the flap down. Adjust by bending the parts to create a comfortable fit.

A springy strap built into the flap keeps these earrings closed.

Pendant Bails

Design Considerations

The bail is the point of connection between a pendant and the cord or chain on which it hangs. Besides being critical to the proper function of the pendant, bails are an opportunity to enhance the design. Consider the location, shape and scale of the bail from the very beginning.

Ideally, the point of contact for a bail is directly above the center of gravity of a pendant. While this is rarely possible, try to be as close to this as possible. To remember this, just visualize what happens when a pendant hangs from the center of the back.

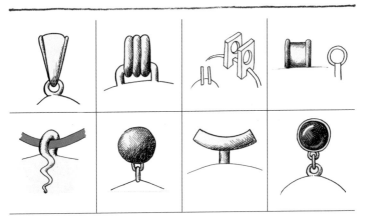

Fold-Down Bail

1. Draw a bead on both ends of a length of wire; hammer them flat and drill a hole in each end.

2. Saw out a piece of sheet with a tongue extending on one side. File this shaft to a round cross section.

3. Form the wire into a loop and rivet it onto the prepared sheet. Bend the loop to one side to do this.

4. Make a U-shaped joint and solder it to the piece.

5. Drill a hole through the joint and sheet and secure them with a pin.

Pin Findings

Pin Findings

Locate pin mechanisms above the central axis to prevent brooches from tipping forward.

The end of the pin should not extend beyond the catch. Position the catch with the opening downward.

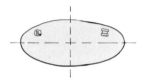

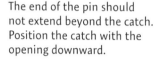

If a pin is too sharp, it will pierce threads and damage fabric. A smooth, bullet-shaped point will find its way between threads. File the proper rounded shape, burnish it to toughen, then polish the pin with rouge.

At rest, the pinstem should be slightly above the catch. This will create a tension that will help keep the pin closed. A similar tension is created by including a stop that holds the stem off the brooch at a slight angle.

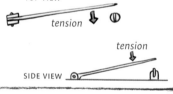

TOP VIEW

tension

tension

SIDE VIEW

Pinstems

Pinstems should be made of a tough metal like low karat gold, nickel silver or stainless steel. Many designs are possible, and each will include a stop that keeps the pin in tension as it fits into the catch. Harden after soldering by twisting the wire.

Pin Catches

Pin catches also come in hundreds of styles, and like pinstems, they can be bought or made. Use a tough metal and engineer a catch that is easy to open on purpose, but that will avoid coming open by accident.

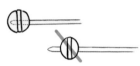

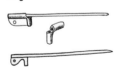

Terminals

This is about as simple as they come: solder one ring into another, then attach that to the chain. For elegant simplicity, it's hard to beat.	Solder a length of tube onto a jump ring, then solder or glue the cord into the tube. Use unusual proportions to create an interesting terminal.	Wrap wire around a mandrel that is slightly smaller than the cord (to allow for spring back). Solder the coils together as you solder a ring into position acrosss the top of the coil.
You'll be able to devise dozens of variations on this style — a length of tubing, capped and fitted with a ring. In this case, saw a jump ring in half to make an interesting hoop.	Tubing can be orna-mented with engrav-ing, file work, mixed metals, and other techniques to make fancy terminals. 	This ending is fab-ricated from wire, first by attaching two pieces to form an X. These were then bent down to make a cage, and secured with two jump rings.
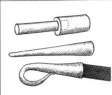 This classic terminal starts with a length of tubing and a wire that makes a snug fit into it. Solder them together, then file to create a smooth taper. Anneal and bend the length into a graceful curve.	 Cut a sheet of thin metal into the form above. File the edges and bend over a nail or similar tool. Close the sides, solder them together, and attach the cord or chain.	 Make a cone from sheet metal and solder a jump ring onto the tip. As shown, this can be embellished, for instance with shot of a contrasting metal.

Barrel Clasps

A successful clasp will:
> be secure.
> inspire confidence.
> be easy to understand and operate.
> contribute to the design, visually and conceptually.
> be easy to adjust and repair.

Toggle Clasps

This classic clasp combines simplicity, versatility and practicality. It's easy to make, relatively easy to use and very secure. The concept lends itself to all sorts of embellishments.

Toggles consist of two parts and while they can be almost any size, the relationship between the parts is important. Both the Ring and the Bar need to be free to pivot, so both have a small loop. The diameter of the Ring (A) is slightly smaller than the distance from the center of the Bar to either end (B). The Bar-plus-small-loop must be able to pass easily through the Ring.

J-Clasp

In this versatile necklace clasp, a piston slides into a sleeve, rotates, and is pushed outward to lock into the hook section of the slot. Though shown in a simple version, this clasp can be embellished.

1. Make or buy two tubes that fit smoothly, one inside the other. Cap the outer tube and attach a loop. This can be fixed or free to rotate.

2. Drill a hole in the outer tube at what will be the end of a J-shaped loop and saw to this. File the edges to make them smooth and parallel.

3. Solder a wire the same size as the slot on the tip of the smaller tube. Cap and attach a loop to the opposite end of the tube.

4. Make a spring from thin, hard-drawn brass wire, a little smaller than the inside diameter of the tube and force it all the way into the tube. The spring pushes the tongue outward, and locks the peg into the end of the slot. →

Box Catches

Basics

> In all these clasps it is important to measure carefully. Make the receiving side first, then make the tongue oversized and file it to achieve a perfect fit.

> The tongue should slide snugly into its bay, with no sloppiness side to side.

> The tongue is usually about 24 gauge. After folding and checking the fit, planish the fold to harden it.

> The amount of squeeze needed for release should be slight. The release distance is determined by, among other things, the length of the snag—keep it just long enough to catch the tongue.

---

1. Make a rectangular frame, typically from 22– or 24–gauge metal. It is important that the corners are square and the sides perfectly parallel.

2. Saw off most of one of the short sides to make the opening for the tongue.

3. Cut a strip of metal for the tongue, twice as long as the box and quite thin. Cut slightly oversize and file to make a perfect fit into the box.

4. Solder a trigger onto the tongue. To center, set dividers by eye to mid-width, then scribe a line from both sides.

5. Solder on the second deck, closing the box. Leave it long enough to make a space for the loop. Polish all parts.

6. Scribe a shallow line across the tongue, making sure it is perpendicular to the edge.

7. Fold the tongue, planish the fold lightly, then pry the tongue up with a blade.

8. Test the fit, filing as needed to make the parts slide together and click. Cut the trigger to its final length and file or saw a few notches for a fingernail grip.

Chainmaking Basics

Making Jump Rings

Wrap a wire around a rod of the chosen size keeping each coil tight to the one before it. Some handy mandrels are nails, dowels, wire and knitting needles. Slide the coil off and cut it with a jeweler's saw or separating disk.

Assembly Sequence

1. Make as many rings as you think will be needed. Solder half the rings closed.

2. Thread a pair of closed rings onto an open ring. Close it and solder the joint. Pick soldering is the most efficient method.

3. Connect two of the three-piece units with a new ring and solder it.

4. Continue joining units of 7, 15, 31, etc. until the chain is the desired length. Pickle only after the assembly is complete.

Polishing Chains

Never polish chains on the buffing wheel! (Unless you have an oversupply of fingers...) Instead, pull the chain taut, and rub it with steel wool, Scotch-Brite, a scratchbrush or a polishing cloth. Use wire or string at each end to allow access to the full length of the chain.

Cutting with a Separating Disk

To cut rings made of thin wire with a separating disk, wrap tape over the coil then cut through tape and wire at the same time. The tape holds the wires steady for the cutting disk.

Should this ring be soldered?

Unsoldered jump rings can look messy and weaken a chain. Sometimes the proper question is "What ratio of wire to ring do I need to provide sufficient strength?" When you won't be soldering them, make jump rings from work-hardened wire.

Cable Chains

Cable

This is the chain we probably think of when we think of chains—
it's the chain we made as kids by interlocking and gluing strips of
construction paper. Variations on this chain alone would provide
enough material for an entire book.

> The proportion of wire to loop will make huge differences.
> Loops can be of different sizes, distributed evenly or randomly.
> Loops can be of contrasting metals.

Hammering – *Method One*

1. Count out half of the jump rings and solder them closed with hard
   solder. Pickle, rinse, and dry, then planish on an anvil. Set these aside.
2. Spread the remaining rings on an anvil and planish each ring to the
   desired shape. Be careful to strike the ring evenly all
   around so the ends remain close together.
3. Use the method described earlier to assemble the
   chain, joining two soldered rings with each open ring.
   Continue until all the rings are used.
4. Replanish as needed to camouflage the solder joints.

Hammering – *Method Two*

1. Make a standard cable chain of round wire as described
   earlier. Pickle, rinse and dry the chain.
2. Working over an edge of an anvil, planish each loop in
   succession. You will need to strike a few blows then turn
   the loop to expose a new section.

Prepared Wires

Cable chains can be made with
wires that are other than round.
These can sometimes be bought,
but all can be made.

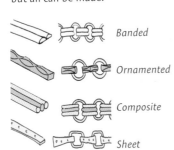

Banded

Ornamented

Composite

Sheet

Elongated

Round loops are the easiest
to make, to open and to close.
Whenever possible, make round
links. After assembling a chain with
soldered links, catch a link on the
tip of round-nose pliers and pull
the handles to stretch the loop.
These can also
be twisted after
stretching by
using two pairs
of pliers.

Woven Chains

Woven Chain

1. Start with a piece of wire about 2 feet long. This chain works in any size, but 22–28 B&S is typical. Bend an EKG-sort of squiggle so the height of each bump is no more than ¾" (19 mm). The number of humps (in this example, 4) will determine the size of the chain. Any number between 3 and 12 is possible.

2. Gather in the loops and wrap them with the short end as if you were tying a bundle. Using pliers, pull the loops into a symmetrical arrangement. This looks a bit like a flower. (Okay, a scrawny, ugly flower.)

3. Feed the long end through a loop (any loop), going from *inside* the bunch *outward*.

4. Slide the end back into the loop it just came out of, and out through the adjacent loop. Put a scribe in the new loop and pull it tight. Note that if it were not for the scribe, the loop would be pulled through and would disappear. That's how you can tell you've got it right.

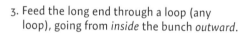

5. Repeat this process, folding new loops upward (along the chain's axis) as you go. Pull each loop tight on the scribe. You can proceed clockwise or counterclockwise, but once you've chosen a direction, stick with it. Continue until there is only about an inch of wire left.

Woven Chains

6. The first step in adding more wire is to make a half stitch. That is, feed the wire back into the loop it is coming out of, but do not send it out the neighboring loop. Feed the end of a 2-foot length of wire into the loop that would have received the next stitch. Twist the old and new ends together and snip off excess wire. Resume weaving, keeping the twist inside the chain.

7. To compress and elongate the weave, anneal the chain and pull it gently through a drawplate.

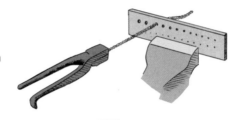

8. To make the chain flexible, anneal the drawn chain, and wrap it around a dowel held in a vise. Pull back and forth vigorously. Anneal and repeat until the chain is pliable.

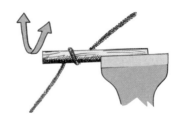

Tips

> Grab the end of the wire with pliers to pull each new loop snug on the scribe.
> Try to keep the loops uniform in size.
> Use wires of various metals for color effects.
> You can make this chain with three, four, five, or more loops. In Step #1 make the number of loops equal to the size chain you want to make. More loops make the chain larger, more intricate in appearance, and hollow.

Loop-in-Loop Chains

The Loop-in-Loop Family

Chains in this family share a common building block—links that are soldered or fused closed before assembly. In most cases, the links are made round and shaped into long ovals before they are slid one into the next. Thanks to Jean Stark, whose excellent book, *Classical Loop-in-Loop Chains and Their Derivatives* provided a lot of this information, used with permission.

Basic Loop-in-Loop

This ancient chain is popular for its versatile beauty. It takes a while to make, but the procedure is simple. Unlike other members of the family, almost any combination of wire size and loop diameter will look attractive.

1. Wrap wire around a rod and cut the rings, typically with small scisssors. In the basic chain almost any wire-to-loop proportion will look good, but the effect can be quite different. For this reason, it's a good idea to make a sample before cutting out too many rings.

2. Bend each loop so the ends come together to make a tight joint. Fuse or solder the rings closed, ideally with an invisible joint. If you use solder, keep the chips as small as possible. Roll a sheet of solder through the mill until the rollers cannot be brought any closer together. Cut this very thin sheet into tiny pieces and use only one on each joint. A biology needle makes a good solder pick.

3. With round-nose pliers, pull each ring into a long oval. Try to avoid stretching the rings; the goal is to achieve uniform size. To maintain a uniform size, some people mark their pliers, either with ink or by filing a small groove.

Loop-in-Loop Chains

4. To start the chain, bend a loop so that the two ends (which we'll call wickets) face each other. Add a twist of wire to make a handle.

5. To weave, bend the tops of the lower loop up and feed a new loop through both wickets. Bend the ends of this new loop up a little to hold it in place.

6. New loops are added this way, always going through the lowest loop possible. It is often necessary to straighten or enlarge loops with a scribe or similar sharp tool as the assembly progresses.

7. When assembly is complete, press each link down onto a tapered point to make the form symmetrical. Rotate and press each link down four times.

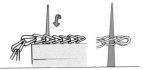

8. To compress and lengthen the chain, pull lightly through a round drawplate. A wooden or plastic drawplate is sufficient for this step. Anneal the chain before drawing.

Suggested Sizes

It's a good idea to make an inch or two of sample chain to confirm the size of wire and loop that will best meet your needs. Here are some points of reference:

Wire size (B&S)	Diameter of mandrel	Finished diameter	Links per inch
22	10 mm	5 mm	13
24	7 mm	4 mm	18
26	6 mm	3½ mm	20
28	5 mm	3 mm	24

Idiot's Delight Chains

Idiot's Delight

1. Make a batch of rings; open half and close the other half. Always open by twisting sideways.

2. Feed an open ring through four closed rings, then close it.

3. Feed a second open ring through the same four and close it. Shading indicates two rings.

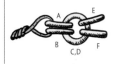

4. Flop two rings back and put a wire or paper clip through them to serve as a handle.

5. Flop E and F to the left and right. Flop C and D forward and backward to expose the lower section of E and F. Slide a needle through here as a place holder.

6. Slip two closed rings (G and H) on an open ring (I) and feed (I) into the space held by the needle. Add a second link (J) beside I and close it.

7. Let the chain droop to allow each link to fall into place. When you lay it out the pattern should emerge.

8. Fold G and H out to expose the lower portion of I and J. Slide the needle through here. This is a repeat of #6.

9. Continue as before, adding an open ring that already has two closed rings on it, and so on.

Sequential Link

Follow 1–7 above. Add two more rings through G and H and close them. These are marked K and L.

Repeat the flopping: K and L to either side, G and H laid apart to expose the bottom section of K and L.

Add an open ring that has two closed rings on it. Then add two more (like K and L) and continue.

Basic Hinges

1. Prepare the object by completing all soldering. Make sure the parts fit together well—it will be more difficult to adjust this after the hinge is in place.

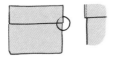

2. Separate the parts and file an angle along the two edges that will take the hinge. Each of these is a 45° angle, which creates a 90° angle when the top is set onto the box.

3. Convert the angled opening to a rounded one (e.g., change a "V" into a "U"). A tapered needle file can do the job, but a parallel round file is much better. An alternative is to use a nail with the same diameter to scrape the groove.

4. Clean the tube to remove any finger oils and tarnish. Measure the length of the hinge and divide this into three or five parts. Use a tube cutting jig to cut the knuckles. Inspect for burs, and remove them with careful filing.

Yes *No*

4A. If you don't have a jig, drill a hole in your benchpin that is precisely at a right angle. Mark the length on tape with a pen, and use this to both cut and file the ends square.

5. Tie the box and lid together with binding wire and prop it so the hinge groove is conveniently angled. Flux, set the knuckles in place, and lay a tiny bit of solder against each knuckle.

6. Gently heat the unit until the flux becomes crusty, then concentrate heat on one side. Bring this up to temperature, easing off as the solder starts to soften. Pull the heat away the instant the solder flows. Repeat on the other side. If you are not certain that the solder has flowed, resist the temptation to give it just another second. Resist!

7. Quench in water, remove the binding wire, and separate the parts. If they stick, gently wiggle them— sometimes there is a phantom join that easily comes apart. Clean up in pickle, and if part of the design, solder on a closure. Repickle, then finish the box with sanding, brassbrushing, patinas, etc. Insert a hinge pin, planish one end to widen it, then pull this into the tube and trim both ends.

Cradle Hinges

Cradle Hinge

This style is especially good for round boxes because the cradle provides increased contact between the parts. Also, this hinge automatically creates a stop to prevent the lid from flopping too far open.

1. Prepare a trough by filing.

2. Buy or make two tubes that telescope together.

3. Cut a piece of the outer tube a bit longer than you think the hinge will be. Cut a slot along the axis of this tube.

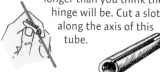

4. Set this tube in position with the sawn slot located as shown, where the box and lid come together. Solder both sides.

5. Cut the entire length on a line that is one-third away from the first slot. The lid will come away from the base.

6. Make another cut, this time removing one-third of the tube. The result is a pair of cradles that are parallel, well attached to both parts, and that fit the knuckles perfectly.

7. Measure and cut hinge knuckles using a jig if available. An odd number is customary.

8. Set a knuckle into the cradle and solder it into place. Visually line this up with the center of the box.

9. Set the box and lid together and mark the location of the first knuckle with file notches on the opposite cradle.

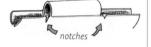

notches

10. Using the notches as guides, solder the other knuckles into their cradles. Check the placement. If it is incorrect, reheat and slide the knuckles as needed. Don't try to correct by grinding... it never works. Pickle, polish, and set the hinge.

Spring Hinges

Coil Spring

Make a hinge in the usual way but leave a space that will be occupied by the spring. This can be accomplished by cutting away one of the knuckles but it will be neater if you plan ahead and leave a space when measuring the knuckles.

The spring is a coil of hard-drawn wire. Depending on the weight of the lid and the fineness of the piece this can be gold, sterling, brass, nickel silver or steel.

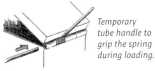

Temporary tube handle to grip the spring during loading.

To assemble the hinge, load the spring into position before inserting the hinge pin. This can be a tricky operation and is easier with two people. The tails of the coil must protrude to make this spring work. Depending on where you put these you can make the lid spring open or snap closed.

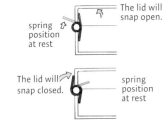

The lid will snap open.

spring position at rest

The lid will snap closed.

spring position at rest

A Compression Spring

This is best used where only a small push is needed. It is common on the covers of pocket watches, for instance. This spring is not in the hinge at all. Somewhere near the hinge is a piece of metal that is pushed down when the lid is closed. When the clasp is released the little tab pushes upward.

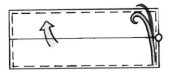

Leaf Springs

A leaf spring is nothing more than a flat bar of springy material—think of a diving board. These can be used in multiples (look under a truck) but for jewelers they are usually nothing more than a toughened piece of metal bent so that it presses against a moving part.

Allow room for the spring to flatten out.

Box Closures

Friction Catches

These are far and away the most common type of clasp, and technically the term covers everything from a cork in a bottle to Tupperware. Friction catches use the natural elasticity of a material to allow parts to rub against each other without breaking. In metals it is important to remember to keep the parts thin enough to move rather than wear away under pressure.

Interior Bezels

A bezel is a thin vertical wall, familiar to jewelers from its use in stonesetting. In the case of a box it can be full or partial and can be attached to either the base or the lid. To tighten a loose bezel, pull it out by rubbing with a burnisher.

Purse Snap

This versatile and ingenious clasp starts with two spheres, each attached to a stem. Bend the wires so the two balls rub against each other as the container closes.

Partial Bezels

Round the top edge of the bezel so it doesn't snag as the box is closed. Bezels can be soldered just inside the edge or they can lie against the entire height of the wall.

← Prepolish this piece

Post

We can think of these as really small partial bezels. On lids that lift off there will need to be at least three posts (and the more, the better). In a hinged box it is typical to have a single thin post directly opposite the hinge. Because of the angle of opening this will need to be kept short.

This variation uses three posts and has the benefit of aligning the lid as it closes. Friction is provided mostly by the edges of the posts rubbing together.

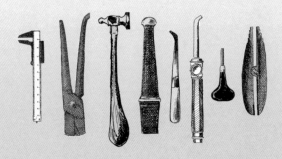

Appendix

Health & Safety

Common Sense

Common sense is your best protection. Even safe procedures can be dangerous if abused. Remember that accidents don't happen only to the other guy. If you feel uncertain about a tool, get help. If you feel ill or dizzy, stop doing what you're doing. If illness persists, contact your state hospital system, Department of Occupational Safety.

While most of the information in this book can apply to metalsmithing on any scale, keep in mind that it is written primarily for work in jewelry studios. It is not intended as a resource for large commercial studios or industry, where other safety requirements may very well exist. For help in this area, contact your state's Office for Occupational Safety and Health Administration (OSHA) or the industrial safety division of your state labor department.

Resources

The National Institute for Occupational Safety and Health (NIOSH) is a vast organization that offers a wide range of services and suggestions. From their website (www.cdc.gov/niosh) you can download or order the *NIOSH Pocket Guide to Chemical Hazards (NPG)*, a thorough reference for conscientious workers. Available as PDF and mobile app.

You'll also find there a list of publications, safety alerts, and information on how you can query a specific problem. NIOSH can also be reached by phone at 800-356-4674 and by fax at 888-232-3299.

First-Aid Kit

Ever notice how the importance of something changes according to need? At this moment a Band-Aid might be unnecessary and therefore far from your mind, but when you really need one, well... that's not the time to go to the store. Here are some suggestions for supplies any jeweler will want *someday*. Take this list along to the drugstore or discount store the next time you go—it will feel good to have this taken care of. Besides, think how much it will shock your mom.

> antiseptic spray
> asprin
> Band-Aids
> burn ointment
> earplugs

> eyewash
> liquid bandage
> styptic pencil
> tweezers (reserved for splinters)

Studio Chemistry

Compound	Effect	Precaution
Acetone	Headache, drowsiness, skin irritation. One of the least toxic solvents.	Adequate ventilation.
Acetylene	Mild narcotic (intoxicant) in small doses. Large doses can cut off oxygen.	Use caution. Check equipment regularly for leaks.
Ammonia	Irritant to eyes, caustic to lungs. Serious when in strong solution.	Use diluted with soap and water.
Aqua Regia	Most caustic of all acids.	Mix carefully, with strong ventilation. Keep in glass, not tightly stoppered.
Asbestos	Made up of fibers the body cannot dissolve; effects take 20–30 years to develop.	Avoid it! Use substitutes.
Benzene	Intoxication, coma, respiratory failure.	Avoid it! Use alternative solvents.
Copper compounds	Oxides can irritate lungs, intestines, eyes and skin.	Ventilate when heating. Wear gloves when handling, e.g., raising.
Cyanides	Mists inhaled or falling on skin are poisonous.	Ventilate well, wear protective clothing. No nude plating.
Fluorides	Can form hydrofluoric acid in the lungs.	Ventilate. Avoid breathing the fumes.
Lead	Damages brain, central nervous system, red blood cells, marrow, liver, kidneys. Fumes are especially dangerous.	Avoid if possible. Ventilate well. Minimize handling, wash hands after touching.
Ketones	Skin, eye, and respiratory tract irritants. Can cause peripheral nerve damage.	Ventilate, wear appropriate respirator. Wear gloves.

Studio Chemistry

Compound	Effect	Precaution
Liver of sulfur	When heated to decomposition, it releases sulfur oxide fumes that react with moisture to form hydrogen sulfide.	Do not allow mixture to come to a boil. All coloring benefits can be obtained from a warm, not hot, solution.
Mercury	Damages brain, nervous system and kidneys.	Avoid fumes and skin contact. Ventilate and wear gloves.
Pitch	Skin irritant when hot.	Wear gloves, avoid heating to a boil.
Platinum	Metal is safe but fumes can cause lung and skin irritation.	Ventilate.
Polyester resins	Skin irritant. Some resins release toxic fumes when mixed with binders.	Wear gloves and ventilate. Store according to directions.
Silver compounds	Absorbed into skin as vapor or dust, these can cause a disease called argyria. Silver dust in eyes can cause blindness.	Wear goggles, gloves and a respirator.
Sulfuric acid & Sparex	Irritates skin and respiratory tract. Damages clothing.	Ventilate. Keep container covered. Neutralize with baking soda and water.
Tellurium	Fumes generated in refining gold, silver, copper and in welding.	Ventilate. Early symptom is "garlic breath," a metallic taste in the mouth.
Toluene a.k.a. Toluol	Causes hallucination, intoxication, lung, brain and red blood cell damage.	Avoid if possible. Ventilate well.
Zinc compounds	Dust and fumes attack the central nervous system, skin and lungs.	Ventilate and wear respirator.

Repetitive Strain Injuries

Repetitive Strain Injuries

Repetitive Strain Injuries (RSI) are a collection of problems centered in the arm, wrist and fingers. As muscles tighten they can become starved for oxygen and overladen with acidic waste products that are normally carried away by the bloodstream. It appears that some people are more prone to RSIs than others. The impact of the activity does not appear to play a major role in the disease—typists and diamond setters are just as likely to suffer as bricklayers and blacksmiths.

Symptoms

> tenderness and pain in your hands and arms
> tingling or numbness in your fingers
> loss of ability to grip objects securely
> sudden locking up of your fingers, hands, or arms

Causes

> repetitive actions, especially actions that are awkward and constricted
> tension and stress
> poor posture

Carpal Tunnel Syndrome (CTS)

This injury is named for a gap in the bones of the wrist that provides a passage for the median nerve in the hand. Strain causes swelling, which in turn, causes pain and numbness.

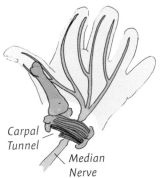

Carpal Tunnel

Median Nerve

Prevention

Beyond a doubt, it is easier to prevent RSIs than to correct a problem once it appears. You don't need expensive equipment or exotic drugs but something a bit more challenging—the discipline to quit working periodically to relax.

Small adjustments can have meaningful benefits.

- wrap punches to make them fatter in the shank
- wear bicycle gloves when hammering
- use a padded bicycle handgrip on your sawframe and file handles
- place rubber pads in front of buffing machines and other places where you stand for extended times

RSI Exercises

> While sitting on the edge of a chair, straighten your spine, and hold your hands out to the side with your palms facing up. Imagine trying to grasp a ball between your shoulder blades.

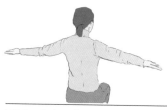

> Hold your hands at your sides and shake them gently and repeatedly for 30 seconds. Time it—it's longer than you might think.

> While sitting down, put your palm on your knee. Lift and hold each finger for a count of 20; repeat for both hands.

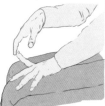

> Put your hands on a table or desk and spread your fingers wide while you count to 10. Relax for a count of 10 and repeat.

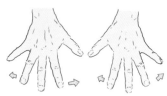

> While standing, reach your hand over your head and down your back to touch your spine. Set your other hand on the elbow of the first (which will be above your head) and gently push it back and down. Repeat for the other arm.

Alloys

Metal	Au	Ag	Cu	Zn	Other	Melting Point		Sp.Grav.
Aluminum					100 Al	660° C	1220° F	2.7
Cartridge brass			70	30		954	1749	8.5
Jeweler's brass			88	12		1030	1886	8.7
Red brass			90	10		1044	1910	8.8
Bronze			96		4 Sn	1060	1945	8.8
Cadmium					100 Cd	321	610	8.7
Copper			100			1083	1981	8.9
Gold (fine)	100					1063	1945	19.3
22K yellow	92	4	4			977	1790	17.3
22K coinage	90	10				940	1724	17.2
18K yellow	75	15	10			882	1620	15.5
18K yellow	75	12½	12½			904	1660	15.7
18K green	75	25				966	1770	15.6
18K rose	75	5	20			932	1710	15.5
18K white	75				25 Pd	904	1660	15.7
14K yellow	58	25	17			802	1476	13.4
14K green	58	35	7			835	1535	13.6
14K rose	58	10	32			827	1520	13.4
14K white	58				42 Pd	927	1700	13.7
10K yellow	42	12	41	5		786	1447	11.6
10K yellow	42	7	48	3		876	1609	11.6
10K green	42	58				804	1480	11.7
10K rose	42	10	48			810	1490	11.6
10K white	42				58 Pd	927	1760	11.8
Iron					100 Fe	1535	2793	7.9
Lead					100 Pb	327	621	11.3
Nickel silver			65	17	18 Ni	1110	2030	8.8
Palladium					100 Pd	1549	2820	12.2
Old pewter					80Pb,20Sn	304	580	9.5
Platinum					100 Pt	1774	3225	21.4
Silver (fine)		100				962	1763	10.6
Sterling		92½	7½			893	1640	10.4
Stainless steel					91 Fe, 9 Cr	1371	2500	7.8
Tin					100 Sn	323	450	7.3
Titanium					100 Ti	1800	3272	4.5
Zinc				100		419	786	7.1

Melting Points

Melting Points

Even if you don't commit to memory all these numbers, it is helpful to have a general understanding of the relative melting points of various materials. Elements have fixed numbers (determined at sea level) but alloys and the miscellaneous materials below show approximations.

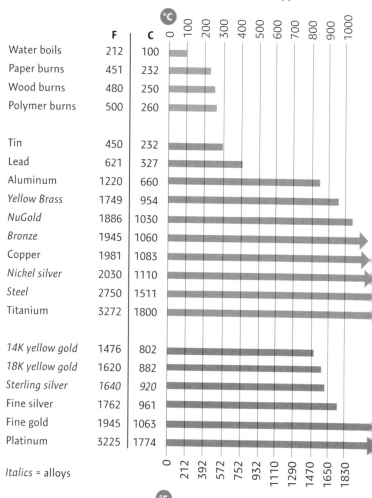

	F	C
Water boils	212	100
Paper burns	451	232
Wood burns	480	250
Polymer burns	500	260
Tin	450	232
Lead	621	327
Aluminum	1220	660
Yellow Brass	1749	954
NuGold	1886	1030
Bronze	1945	1060
Copper	1981	1083
Nickel silver	2030	1110
Steel	2750	1511
Titanium	3272	1800
14K yellow gold	1476	802
18K yellow gold	1620	882
Sterling silver	1640	920
Fine silver	1762	961
Fine gold	1945	1063
Platinum	3225	1774

Italics = alloys

Conversion Factors

Converting one measurement to another

We all know that 1 foot equals 12 inches—that's the kind of conversion you can do with the numbers shown here. To convert the unit in bold to an alternate measurement, multiply by the number shown.

Carats (ct)

to grains	x	3.0865
to grams	x	0.2
to milligrams	x	200

Grains (gr)

to carats	x	0.324
to grams	x	0.0648
to milligrams	x	64.8
to ounce avoir	x	0.00228
to ounce troy	x	0.00208
to pennyweight	x	0.04167

Grams (g)

to carat	x	5
to grains	x	15.4324
to ounce avoir	x	0.03527
to ounce troy	x	0.03215
to pennyweight	x	0.64301

Kilograms (kg)

to ounce avoir	x	35.274
to ounce troy	x	32.1507
to pennyweight	x	643.015
to pound avoir	x	2.2046
to pound troy	x	2.6792

Avoirdupois ounce (oz, avoir)

to grains	x	437.5
to grams	x	28.3495
to oz, troy	x	0.91146
to pennywght	x	18.291
to lb, troy	x	0.07595

Troy ounce (oz, troy)

to grains	x	480
to grams	x	31.1035
to ounce avoir	x	1.0971
to pennyweight	x	20
to pound avoir	x	0.06857

Pennyweights (dwt)

to grains	x	24
to grams	x	1.5551
to oz, avoir	x	0.05486

Pound avoirdupois (lb. avoir.)

to grains	x	7000
to grams	x	453.59
to kilograms	x	0.4536
to oz, troy	x	14.5833

Pound troy (lb. troy)

to gram	x	373.242
to kilogram	x	0.3732
to ounce avoir	x	13.165
to ounce troy	x	12.000
to pound avoir	x	0.82286

Feet (')

| to centimeters | x | 30.48 |
| to meters | x | 0.3048 |

Meters (m)

| to feet | x | 3.2808 |
| to inches | x | 0.03937 |

Inches (")

to centimeters	x	2.54
to meters	x	0.0254
to millimeters	x	25.4

Cubic centimeters (cu cm)

| to cubic inches | x | 0.061 |
| to US fl oz | x | 0.0338 |

Cubic inches (cu in)

to cu cm	x	16.387
to liters	x	0.01639
to US fl oz	x	0.554

US gallons

| to liters | x | 3.785 |
| to cubic inches | x | 231 |

Weight of Sheet

Weight per square inch in ounces or pennyweights (dwt)

mm	inch	B&S	fine silver (oz)	sterling silver (oz)	fine gold (dwts)	10K gold (dwts)	14K gold (dwts)	18K gold (dwts)	fine platinum (oz)
6.54	.2576	2	1.42	1.41	52.5	31.4	35.5	42.3	2.91
5.19	.2043	4	1.12	1.12	41.6	24.9	28.1	33.6	2.31
4.11	.1620	6	0.894	0.884	33.0	19.8	22.3	26.6	1.83
3.26	.1285	8	0.709	0.701	26.2	15.7	17.7	21.1	1.45
2.59	.1019	10	0.562	0.556	20.8	12.4	14.0	16.7	1.15
2.05	.0808	12	0.446	0.441	16.5	9.85	11.1	13.3	0.913
1.63	0.0641	14	0.354	0.350	13.1	7.81	8.82	10.5	0.724
1.29	0.0508	16	0.281	0.277	10.4	6.21	7.00	8.35	0.574
1.02	0.0403	18	0.223	0.220	8.20	4.91	5.55	6.62	0.455
0.813	0.0320	20	0.176	0.174	6.51	3.90	4.40	5.25	0.361
0.645	0.253	22	0.140	0.138	5.16	3.09	3.49	4.216	0.286
0.511	0.0201	24	0.111	0.110	4.09	2.45	2.77	3.30	0.227
0.404	0.0154	26	0.088	0.087	3.24	1.94	2.19	2.62	0.180
0.330	0.0126	28	0.070	0.069	2.58	1.54	1.74	2.08	0.143
0.254	0.100	30	0.055	0.055	2.04	1.22	1.38	1.65	0.113

Weight of Round Wire

Weight per foot of wire in ounces or pennyweights (dwt)

mm	inch	B&S	fine silver (oz)	sterling silver (oz)	fine gold (dwts)	10K gold (dwts)	14K gold (dwts)	18K gold (dwts)	fine platinum (oz)
6.54	0.2576	2	3.45	3.41	128	76.3	86.1	104	7.07
5.19	0.2043	4	2.17	2.14	80.1	48.0	54.2	64.6	4.45
4.11	0.1620	6	1.36	1.35	50.4	30.2	34.1	40.6	2.80
3.26	0.1285	8	0.856	0.848	31.6	19.0	21.4	25.6	1.76
2.59	0.1019	10	0.541	0.534	20.0	11.9	13.5	16.1	1.11
2.05	0.0808	12	0.339	0.335	12.6	7.50	8.47	10.1	0.695
1.63	0.0641	14	0.214	0.211	7.78	4.72	5.33	6.36	0.437
1.29	0.0508	16	0.135	0.132	4.96	2.97	3.35	4.00	0.275
1.02	0.0403	18	0.085	0.084	3.11	1.87	2.11	2.51	0.173
0.813	0.0320	20	0.053	0.053	1.96	1.17	1.33	1.58	0.109
0.643	0.025	22	0.034	0.033	1.23	0.738	0.833	0.994	0.068
0.511	0.0201	24	0.021	0.021	0.775	0.464	0.524	0.625	0.043
0.404	0.0154	26	0.013	0.013	0.488	0.292	0.330	0.393	0.027
0.330	0.0126	28	0.008	0.008	0.306	0.184	0.287	0.247	0.017
0.254	0.0100	30	0.005	0.005	0.193	0.115	0.130	0.155	0.010

Equivalents & Conversions

Equivalent Numbers

B&S	mm	inches		drill #
0	8.5	.325	$^{21}/_{64}$	
1	7.34	.289	$^{9}/_{32}$	
2	6.52	.257	$^{1}/_{4}$	
3	5.81	.229	$^{7}/_{32}$	1
4	5.18	.204	$^{13}/_{64}$	6
5	4.62	.182	$^{3}/_{16}$	15
6	4.11	.162	$^{5}/_{32}$	20
7	3.66	.144	$^{9}/_{64}$	27
8	3.25	.128	$^{1}/_{8}$	30
9	2.90	.114		
10	2.59	.102		38
11	2.31	.091	$^{3}/_{32}$	43
12	2.06	.081	$^{5}/_{64}$	46
13	1.83	.072		50
14	1.63	.064	$^{1}/_{16}$	51
15	1.45	.057		52
16	1.30	.051		54
17	1.14	.045	$^{3}/_{64}$	55
18	1.02	.040		56
19	0.914	.036		60
20	0.812	.032	$^{1}/_{32}$	65
21	0.711	.028		67
22	0.635	.025		70
23	0.558	.022		71
24	0.508	.020		74
25	0.457	.018		75
26	0.406	.016	$^{1}/_{64}$	77
27	0.355	.014		78
28	0.304	.012		79
29	0.279	.011		80
30	0.254	.010		

Metal Conversions

These factors allow you to calculate the weight of a known object in an alternate metal, as in "How much would this sterling ring weigh in 18K gold?"

To change this:	to this,	multiply by this:
Sterling	18K gold	1.48
	14K gold	1.248
	10K gold	1.104
	platinum	2.046
	fine silver	1.015
Brass	18K gold	1.885
	14K gold	1.589
	10K gold	1.406
	fine silver	1.273
	sterling	1.21
18KY Gold	18KW gold	1.064
	14K gold	0.842
	10K gold	0.745
	platinum	0.727
	sterling	0.675
14KY Gold	18K gold	1.157
	14KW gold	1.035
	10K gold	0.884
	fine silver	0.791
	sterling	0.801
Platinum	18K gold	0.722
	14K gold	0.625
	10K gold	0.528
	fine silver	0.494
	sterling	0.483

Temperature Conversions

Celsius to Fahrenheit

> Multiply the degrees C times 9.
> Divide this number by 5.
> Add 32

Fahrenheit to Celsius

> Subtract 32 from the degrees F.
> Multiply this number by 5.
> Divide by 9.

°C	°F	°C	°F
0	32	650	1202
50	122	675	1247
75	167	700	1382
100	212	725	1337
125	257	750	1382
150	302	775	1427
175	347	800	1470
200	392	825	1517
225	437	850	1562
250	482	875	1607
275	527	900	1652
300	572	925	1697
325	617	950	1742
350	662	975	1787
375	707	1000	1832
400	752	1025	1877
425	797	1050	1922
450	842	1075	1967
475	887	1100	2012
500	932	1125	2057
525	977	1150	2102
550	932	1175	2147
575	1067	1200	2192
600	1112	1225	2237
625	1157	1250	2282

°F	°C	°F	°C
32	0	1300	704
100	38	1350	732
150	66	1400	760
200	93	1450	788
250	121	1500	816
300	149	1550	843
350	177	1600	871
400	204	1650	871
450	232	1700	927
500	260	1750	954
550	288	1800	982
600	316	1850	1010
650	343	1900	1038
700	371	1950	1066
750	399	2000	1093
800	427	2050	1121
850	454	2100	1149
900	482	2150	1177
950	510	2200	1204
1000	538	2250	1232
1050	566	2300	1260
1100	593	2350	1288
1150	621	2400	1316
1200	649	2450	1343
1250	677	2500	1371

Phase Diagrams

Silver/Copper Phase Diagram

The left edge represents 100% silver. The point marked A indicates its melting point at 1761° F (960.5° C). The right edge represents 100% copper, whose melting point is shown at B. Reading across the graph, the percentage of copper is increased as the silver is decreased. Halfway across is an alloy of equal parts of the two metals. The bottom edge of the graph is the lowest temperature shown, in this case 400° C. Each phase diagram will use different temperature ranges, choosing the range that is pertinent to the alloy being displayed.

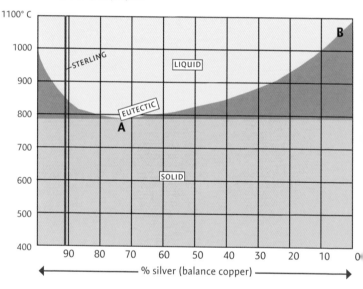

To fill in the graph, laboratory tests are made for many alloys, first a mixture of 99 parts silver to 1 part copper, then 98:2, 97:3, and so forth. These tests determine the temperature at which the alloy is no longer solid (the *solidus*) and the temperature at which it is totally liquid (the *liquidus*). These are plotted on the graph and yield the freezing curve, shown here as the boundary between yellow and blue regions, dipping down to nothing at the left of center (**A**). This tells us that of all possible mixtures of these two metals, a combination of 71.9% silver and 28.1% copper has the lowest freezing point (1438° F, 781° C). Sterling, an alloy of 7.5% copper and 92.5% silver, is indicated on the diagram by the vertical redline near the left edge: the graph shows that its melting point is 1640° F (893° C). The blue area is neither solid nor liquid... "slushy."

Copyright Basics

Intellectual Property Laws

Category	Description	Example
Copyright	Protects writings, designs, expression, and images. This is a federal protection.	Mickey Mouse
Trademark	A graphic image and/or words associated with a specific product.	Nike athletic equipment
Patent	Registered ownership of a device or process that is proven to be not obvious to others in the field.	When you invent a better mousetrap, you may patent it.
Trade Secrets	Similar to patent but easier to acquire. Often used while a patent is pending.	Can't tell you. It's a secret.

Common Assumptions

> It doesn't have a © mark so it's okay to use it.   Wrong.

> I'm not making money on this, so it's okay to use it.   Wrong.

> I got it off the Internet so all rights are waived.   Wrong.

> I'm using only a small portion for review or parody
and I'll make it clear I'm not the author/designer.   Okay.

> Copyright is lost if you don't defend it.   Wrong.

> If a work is reproduced for education, the usual   Wrong.
copyright rules do not apply. *(Many copyright holders,
however, allow limited use in legitimate academic situations.)*

Copyright

Copyright is automatic as soon as a work is in a "fixed form"—typed, drawn, printed, etc. The © notation is not necessary but it is required before you file an infringement suit.

Unless you are specifically given permission or know that a work is in the public domain, seek permission before you use something that you did not create.

Patents

Patents fall into two categories: utility (the way a widget works) and design (the way the widget looks). Patents are given only to two-dimensional materials; not a clasp but a drawing of a clasp. Securing a patent is often a long and costly procedure because it is necessary to prove that no one has had the idea before.

Toolmaking

Phase Transformation

An alloy of about one percent carbon and 99 percent iron yields a material that has the ability to exist in two very different crystalline states, one relatively malleable and the other quite hard. In ancient times, this seemed like magic. It still seems like magic. The next page describes the two-step process of transformation as it is done on a stamping tool. Bear in mind that with this information you can make any edge-holding or impact tool, which includes things like knives, plane blades, scissors, cigar cutters, chisels and lots more.

Spark Test

Before spending time on a tool, be sure you're working with a hardenable material. Mild steel (also called low carbon steel) contains 0.15–0.3% carbon, an amount that is insufficient to cause hardening. To test an unknown piece of material, hold it against a grinding wheel. Mild steel gives dull, round, orange sparks, while tool steel throws bright, star-like sparks that split into multipointed bursts at the tip.

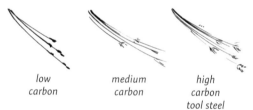

| low carbon | medium carbon | high carbon tool steel |

Tempering Colors

Ink on paper cannot accurately convey the colors you'll see in the studio, but these approximations will inform your observations.

°C	°F	Properties	Uses
200–225	400–445	hard, little flexibility	drill bits
225–265	445–590	hard, less brittle	punches
265–300	490–535	hard, increased flexibility	chisels
300–325	535–580	flexible but holds edge	thick blades
325–350	580–650	medium hard, flexible	thin blades
350–500	650–900	not hard	springs

Hardening & Tempering

Process

. Tool steel is sold in its annealed state, but if you are recycling a worn tool, the first step is to anneal it. Heat the steel to bright red and cool it as slowly as possible. Bury the hot steel in sand or ashes to achieve a slow cooling. A second-best alternative is to set a firebrick onto the hot steel to hold in the heat.

. Shape the tool by forging, sawing, grinding and filing. Forging must be done while the steel is red hot. Do not strike after the color has gone or the steel may crack. When making a patterned tool such as a stamp, check the image by pressing it into clay.

. Harden the tool by heating it to glowing red and quenching it immediately in oil or brine. Hold small tools in tweezers and set large pieces on a brick. Punches are usually hardened only an inch or two up from the stamping end. The goal here is to convert the pearlite stage into martensite. Because this phase is nonmagnetic, at proper temperature, a magnet will not stick.

. Check for hardness by stroking a file across the tool. If the hardening was successful, the file will slide across the steel and make a glassy sound.

. Remove the gray oxide scale with fine sandpaper so you will be able to see the colors of the next step.

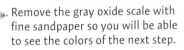

. Reduce brittleness by heating in a step called *drawing the temper* (a.k.a. drawing or tempering). This can be done with a torch or, for small pieces, on a hot plate. Go slowly, letting heat travel from a thick section to a thinner one. The higher the temperature the more flexible the steel will become. This flexibility comes at the cost of hardness, however. The states at the top of the list have maximum hardness but they are also quite brittle. At the bottom of the chart the steel is less brittle, but not as hard.

Suggested Reading

The Art of Stamping
Matthieu Cheminée
Brynmorgen Press, Maine. 2019

Amulets and Superstitions
E. A. Wallis Budge
Dover, New York. 1978 (orig. 1930)

Centrifugal or Lost Wax Jewelry Casting for Schools, Tradesmen
Murray Bovin
Bovin, Forest Hills, New York. 1971

The Curious Lore of Precious Stones
George Kunz
Dover, New York. 1971 (orig. 1913)

Design and Creation of Jewelry
Robert vonNeuman
Chilton, Radnor, PA. 1966, rev. 1972

Rings for the Finger
George Kunz
Dover, New York. 1973 (orig. 1917)

Foldforming
Charles Lewton-Brain
Brynmorgen Press, Maine. 2008

Form Emphasis For Metalsmiths
Heikki Sëppa
Kent State Press, Kent, Ohio. 1978

The Jeweler's Bench Reference
Harold O'Connor
Dunconor, Taos, NM. 1977

The Jewelry Engraver's Manual
Hardy & Allen
Van Nostrand, New York. 1954, 1976

Introduction to Precious Metals
Mark Grimwade
Brynmorgen Press, Maine. 2009

Jewelry Workshop Safety Report
Charles Lewton-Brain
Brain Press Ltd.
Alberta, Canada. 1998

Metalwork and Enameling
Herbert Maryon
Dover, New York. 1971 (orig, 1912)

Metal Techniques for Craftsmen
Oppi Untracht
Doubleday, New York. 1968

Jewelry, Concepts and Design
Oppi Untracht
Doubleday, New York. 1982

Professional Jewelry Making
Alan Revere
Brynmorgen Press, Maine. 2018

Theory & Practice of Goldsmithing
Erhard Brepohl
Brynmorgen Press, Maine. 2001

Creative Metal Forming
Betty Helen Longhi & Cynthia Eid
Brynmorgen Press, Maine. 2013

Circle Divider

Use this tool to divide a circle into uniform parts. Center the work on the target below and make marks at the selected intervals.

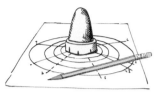

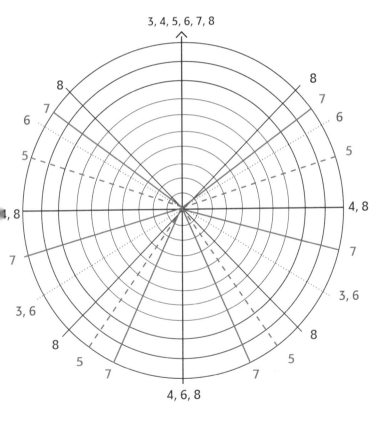

Photographing Jewelry

Tips

Photographing small reflective objects presents two problems. Because the camera is close to the work, depth of field becomes critical. To keep both the foreground and background in focus, it is necessary to keep the lens opening (f-stop) small, (e.g., f–16). To allow enough light to reach the film through such a small opening, a long exposure time is needed. To keep the camera steady for the length of time required, use a tripod. Most digital cameras include a setting for close-up work. Experiment to figure out which settings work for you. If all else fails, read the manual.

It's possible to shoot jewelry in daylight with the appropriate film, but greater consistency is possible when using lights. Flood lights are usually mounted in aluminum reflectors and should be covered with a diffusing material to spread the light outward. Tissue paper will work, but there is a fire hazard because the bulbs get hot. Frosted acrylic, cotton fabric, or sailcloth are better alternatives. To properly illuminate the work and avoid shadows, light should come from both sides and sometimes from above. Use pieces of white foam core to shield, shade and bounce light. To avoid the reflection of the camera and photographer, shoot through a piece of white cardboard with a hole cut out for the lens.

Scale

Scale is important in translating an object into a photograph. In rare cases, a common object like a coin can be set beside the piece, but this usually creates a distraction. Instead, the relationship between the object and the picture area is used to provide a sense of scale.

NO   YES

Background Material

It's easy to forget that a close-up photo is like a magnifying glass. Materials that look good to the naked eye become a jungle of lint, lines, and flaws when viewed close up. Medium values of colored paper make good background surfaces. Color-Aid paper (available at an art supply store) is especially rich looking.

Photo Booth

White fabric, thin paper, or plastic. Stretch fabric or translucent paper over a frame; don't let either get hot enough to ignite.

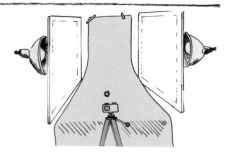

Online Resources

Organizations

snagmetalsmith.org	Society of North American Goldsmiths
craftcouncil.org	American Craft Council
silversmithing.com	Society of American Silversmiths
isgb.org	Int'l. Society of Glass Beadmakers
abana.org	Artist/Blacksmith Association
copper.org	Copper Development Association
cdc.gov/niosh	Nat'l. Institute for Occupational Safety
ganoksin.com	Huge collection of resource for jewelers
metalclaytoday.com	Resources for the metal clay community
www.acj.org.uk	Support and resources for jewelers

Suppliers

castaldo.com	Rubber mold materials
omega.com	Electronic devices, pyrometers, etc.
parawire.com	Assortment of metal wires
AdvantageLumber.com	Wood
woodworkerssource.net	Wood and woodworking equipment
woodcraft.com	Wood and woodworking supplies
tapplastics.com	Supplier of plastics and related supplies
orascoptic.com	Wearable microscopes (dentistry)
knifemaking.com	Steel, handle materials and tools
usaknifemaker.com	Steel, handle materials and tools
goldleafcompany.com	Gold leaf
artessentialsofnewyork.com	Gold leaf materials and instruction

Suppliers

Jewelry Supplies

Allcraft Jewelry Supply
135 W 29th St. Rm 205
New York, NY 10001
  allcraftusa.com

800-645-7124
212-279-7077

Contenti
515 Naragansett Park Dr.
Providence, RI 02861
  contenti.com

800-343-3364
800-651-1887 fax
401-305-3000
401-305-3005 fax

Gesswein
255 Hancock Ave.
PO Box 3998
Bridgeport, CT 06605
  gesswein.com

800-243-4466
888-454-4377 fax
203-366-5400
203-366-3953 fax

Grobet USA
750 Washington Ave.
Carlstadt, NJ 07072
  grobetusa.com

800-847-4188
800-243-2432 fax
201-939-6700
201-939-3099 fax

Metalliferous
2-8 Central Ave.
East Orange, NJ 07018
  metalliferous.com

888-944-0909
212-944-0909

Otto Frei
126 Second St.
Oakland, CA 94607
  ofrei.com

800-772-3456
800-900-3734 fax
510-832-0355
510-834-6217 fax

Rio Grande
7500 Bluewater NW
Albuquerque, NM 87121
  riogrande.com

800-545-6566
800-965-2329 fax
505-839-3300

Suppliers

Specialty Suppliers

David H. Fell & Co Inc   800-822-1996
6009 Bandini Blvd.   323-722-9992
City of Commerce, CA 90040
   dhfco.com

Gun Bluing source:
GSM Outdoors   877-269-8490
PO Box 535189
Grand Prairie, TX 75053
   birchwoodcasey.com

Hauser & Miller Co   800-462-7447
10950 Lin-Valle Drive   800-535-3829 fax
St. Louis, MO 63123   314-487-1311
   hauserandmiller.com

Hoover & Strong   800-759-9997
10700 Trade Road   804 794-3700
Richmond, VA 23236   800-616-9997 fax
   hooverandstrong.com

Micro Fasteners   800-892-6917
13 S. Bank St.   610-438-6177
Easton, PA 18042
   www.microfasteners.com

Reactive Metals Studio   800-876-3434
Box 890   928-634-3434
Clarkdale, AZ 86324   928-634-6734 fax
   reactivemetals.com

United Precious Metal   800-999-3463
2781 Townline Road   800-533-6657 fax
Alden, NY 14004
   unitedpmr.com

Index

Index

Index

Index

Complete Metalsmith was composed on a Macintosh G4 computer using InDesign 2.0. We are proud to premier this font, called Expo Sans, designed by Mark Jamra, www.typeculture.com